Clownfish as Pets

Clownfish Owner's Manual

Clownfish care, health and feeding all included

by

Raymond Rodsdale

Published by: AAX Publishing

Table of Contents

Table of Contents 3

Chapter 1: Introduction 4

Chapter 2: Clownfish basics 6

Chapter 3: Clownfish behaviour...17

Chapter 4: Buying your Clownfish 21

Chapter 5: What you need to buy for your Clownfish 26

Chapter 6: Setting up the aquarium..28

Chapter 7: Water and other parameters....................................51

Chapter 8: Introducing Clownfish and other creatures into the tank 58

Chapter 9: Caring for your Clownfish 63

Chapter 10: Feeding your Clownfish 76

Chapter 11: Health management...79

Chapter 12: Breeding Clownfish..114

Chapter 13: Prices, costs & where to buy Clownfish 126

Chapter 14: Conclusion..129

Chapter 1: Introduction

The Clownfish has featured in marine tanks for many years but the Pixar film "Finding Nemo" really made this colourful little fish a hugely popular aquarium inhabitant. There are no fewer than 28 species to delight the aquarist and these fish are also bred very successfully in captivity, including by hobbyists.

This book will introduce you to these delightful fish by looking at the different species, discussing their appearance and biology, typical Clownfish behaviour, their feeding requirements, and what makes these attractive fish both fascinating and unique.

It will also tell you what you need to know in order to decide whether or not this is the pet for you and, if it is, where to buy one, how to select your Clownfish, what you need to buy before you bring it home, and how to take proper care of it.

The hobbyist also has to know what these fish need with regards to their environment. All the necessary equipment and water and other parameters are examined as the quality of the water and the general environment has a crucial bearing on the health and happiness of Clownfish.

Like all fish, the Clownfish is unfortunately susceptible to a number of different types of bacterial, parasitic and fungal infections and infestations. Anyone who is serious about having a marine tank needs to know what to look for and how to deal with common fish ailments.

This book contains helpful information on their mating behaviour, spawning and on caring for the hatchlings or fry for those who are interested in breeding one or more of the Clownfish species.

Other areas of discussion are the fish and anemones that the Clownfish gets on with. It's important to only combine species that are compatible so you don't have to deal with aggression and bullying between fish. There is also discussion of suitable companion invertebrates that will share the tank with the fish.

Please note that some of the information in this book is not specific to the Clownfish but can be applied to all marine or saltwater aquarium fish. I hope that you find this book both useful and fun to read!

Chapter 2: Clownfish basics

1) Clownfish overview

The Clownfish (*Amphiprioninae*) is also known as the anemone fish. These pretty little fish grow to a length of 4 to 7 inches or 10 to 18 centimetres.

It is said that the name "clown" is thanks to the waddle-like swimming style. Another, and perhaps more understandable, version of the origin of their name is that it is derived from the bold bands of white or black running over their colourful bodies that are reminiscent of the face paint of circus clowns.

They originate in the Indian and Pacific Oceans but they are found in and around tropical coral reefs and prefer warmer waters. The waters they are found in include the Red Sea and in the Great Barrier Reef off the coast of Australia.

These adaptable fish are found living in reefs, sheltered reefs, in shallow seas and even in some lagoons. This means that they can live in both salt and fresh water! The only places you will not find Clownfish are the Atlantic, Caribbean and the Mediterranean.

In addition to the wide range of habitats and locations, they are also found in different shapes and a wide range of colours; not all Clownfish are orange and white! In fact there are no fewer than 28 recognised breeds of this fish.

They are omnivores that mainly feed on zooplankton, algae and small molluscs. They also eat 'leftovers' or undigested food particles released by their host anemone. It is their symbiotic relationship with sea anemones that is one of the features that make these such unique and fascinating fish.

2) Life span or expectancy

In the wild, the Clownfish has a life expectancy of between 6 and 10 years. Like most living creatures, these fish have enemies. The primary predators are larger fish, sharks and eels. Their best defence against predation is to retreat into the stinging tentacles of the host anemone. When they are kept in tanks or aquariums they generally live for only 3 to 5 years. There have been records of Clownfish living for 20 years or more in captivity. However, these individual fish are certainly the exception and not the rule.

The main threat to these fish in the wild is human beings. As stated above, thanks to the 2003 animated film "Finding Nemo" there is now a huge demand for Clownfish for aquariums and tanks.

3) Clownfish anatomy

Basics:

Like all fish, the Clownfish has a head, body, tail and fins. As with most, the two eyes are set on either side of the head, as are the nostrils or nares.

Gills:

Another feature shared with other fish is the gills through which they breathe. The gills are located on either side of the body, just behind the head and are curved. Most fish have 8 gill slits (4 per side) and the gills inside them function like lungs. The covering over the gills are called the operculum.

The gills are complex structures and they absorb oxygen from the water that passes over them. Again similar to lungs, carbon dioxide is released from the gills. When a fish opens and closes its mouth it is actually pumping water in so it can flow over the gills.

In addition to the absorption of oxygen, which is essential to life, the gills also regulate the amount of salt or sodium absorbed by these marine or salt-water fish. Their fresh water cousins need help with this too.

Within the gill itself there are highly specialised cells called, appropriately, chloride cells. These cells are able to excrete the excess salt in the fish's body. Fresh water fish, not surprisingly, have far fewer of these cells in their gills.

Fins:

Clownfish also have the standard range of fins. Each fin in turn serves a different purpose or enables the fish to move in a certain way:

- The dorsal fins are located on the back of the fish and their purpose is to help fish maintain balance and stability when they swim. The rear dorsal fin is soft whereas the larger, front dorsal fin in spiny and more rigid.

- The ventral, or pelvic, fins are found in the pelvic region of the fish. Like the dorsal fins, the pectorals promote stability and balance.

- The pectoral fins are located on either side of the fish, just behind the operculum. They allow side-to-side movements and allow the fish to manoeuvre through the water.

- The caudal fin is also called the tail. This fin is larger than the others and its purpose is to propel the fish through the water.

Mucous:

The mucous they are covered with – and why they are – is the first point of difference between the Clownfish and most other fish. The "why" is to protect the Clownfish from being stung by the sea anemone it calls home! It was thought at first that these colourful little fish were immune to anemone stings. It is now clear that they are not. It is the slimy layer that keeps them safe from the anemone venom or toxins.

This slimy mucous covers the entire adult fish and while there is no debate that it is there, scientists are still debating where it comes from or how it is created and its purpose. There are two primary theories.

The first theory is that the fish produces the mucous and that it contains chemicals of some sort that prevents the sea anemone from stinging the fish. It is also thought by some that this mucous is sugar-based and not protein-based. This would account for the fact that the anemones don't fire their stings, called nematocysts, at the Clownfish; they don't perceive them as food or protein.

The second theory is that the Clownfish rubs itself (very carefully and quickly) against the anemone's tentacles and smears itself with mucous from the anemone in the process. In other words, the fish does not produce the mucous but uses the anemone's own mucous as camouflage or to persuade the anemone that it is not a separate creature or food.

A third explanation of how the Clownfish is able to live unharmed amongst the stinging tentacles of the anemone has nothing to do with the mucous that coats these fish and has everything to do with the way they move. Evidence for this hypothesis is that juveniles have no mucous covering but still live safely amongst anemones. Those who promote this view state that it is the nature of the fish's dance-like, wiggling movements that signal to the anemone that they are not food.

There is some evidence for all three theories and it may be that all are true or partially so, given there are no fewer than 28 species of Clownfish and a variety of anemone hosts.

Gender:

Another most unusual aspect of these fish is their gender or sex. The Clownfish is what is known as a sequential hermaphrodite: Clownfish all begin life as males.

These fish live in schools that consist of one female and many males. The female is the largest and the most dominant. Below the female in the Clownfish hierarchy is the largest and most aggressive male. It is only this male that is permitted to breed with the female.

If the female dies the dominant male undergoes an astonishing transformation. He will gain weight and increase in size and become a female! This new female assumes the lead or dominant position in the school and then selects a mate.

It's believed that this ability to change sex or gender is because the Clownfish never moves far from the sea anemone that it lives in. This static or stay-at-home lifestyle means that it would be very difficult to find a mate or breeding partner.

4) Clownfish and sea anemones

Their symbiotic, or mutualistic, relationship with the sea anemone is the other distinguishing feature of these little fish. A symbiotic relationship is one that provides significant benefits to both parties. A dozen or even more fish of varying ages may live in the same anemone as long as the fish are the same species of Clownfish.

However, it is important to note that not all sea anemones are suitable or willing Clownfish landlords. In addition, specific species are found paired with certain types of anemone. The 10 anemones that are host to these fish are:

- Bubble Tip Anemone (*Entacmaea quadricolor*)
- Beaded Sea Anemone (*Heteractis aurora*)
- Magnificent Sea Anemone (*Heteractis magnifica*)
- Delicate Sea Anemone (*Heteractis malu*)

- Long Tentacle Anemone (*Macrodactyla doreensis*)
- Giant Carpet Anemone (*Stichodactyla gigantean*)
- Merten's Carpet Anemone (*Stichodactyla mertensi*)
- Adhesive Sea Anemone (*Cryptodendrum adhaesivum*)
- Sebae Anemone (*Heteractis crispa*)
- Saddle Anemone (*Stichodactyla haddoni*).

Once paired with an anemone, the Clownfish will live amongst the stinging tentacles of the host anemone for their entire lives. Most Clownfish stay within 2 to 4 inches or 5 to 10 centimetres of the host anemone at all times.

What the anemone offers the Clownfish

The Clownfish enjoys several advantages thanks to their anemone host:

1. They are protected from many predators

2. They get food in the form of particles left behind by the anemone and even dead tentacles

3. The stinging tentacles keep the nest site safe

4. The aeration of the water around it improves the fish's metabolism and respiration.

What the Clownfish offers the anemone

Some would argue that the anemone enjoys even more benefits from the symbiotic relationship than the fish does. These include:

a. They are protected from predation by other small fish and parasites

b. They obtain extra nutrients from the Clownfish's excretions

c. The nitrogen released and the aeration of the water caused by the fish's movement improves metabolism and stimulates growth and respiration

d. The colourful little fish may even attract fish to the anemone that it then stings and eats.

Clownfish that are in captivity, however, don't have to have a sea anemone host. In fact, unless one is 100% sure about which anemone to get and how to care for it, it is much better not to get one!

Fish in captivity will usually readily adapt to a suitable substitute such as a rock or piece of coral that will provide it with shelter.

5) *The history of the Clownfish as a pet*

Although it had featured regularly in tanks and aquariums, the Clownfish was not in great demand until Pixar Studios released the animated film "Finding Nemo" in 2013. This very popular movie told of the adventures of a young Clownfish.

It is estimated that these fish make up approximately 42% of the marine ornamental trade globally. Of these 25% are fish that have been bred in captivity. The fact that the majority of fish are captured in the wild has resulted in reduced numbers. However, the species is not under threat.

6) *Types of Clownfish*

There are now 30 known species of Clown or anemone fish. In order to make them easier to describe and understand they have been grouped into 6 "complexes" or categories:

1. **Percula Complex**: This species is common in aquariums and is being successfully bred in captivity. The fish in this complex are:

    • Percula Clownfish (*Amphiprion percula*) or True Percula Clownfish. The standard fish has the classic markings: orange with the white markings. A new variety has been developed by breeders. It is called the Picasso Clownfish or Picasso Percula Clownfish. Instead of the usual bands

Chapter 3: Clownfish behaviour

1) Social behaviour

Even the less aggressive species of Clownfish become territorial when it comes to their host. Whether it is a sea anemone, rock or piece of coral, a Clownfish will aggressively defend their host against intruders of any kind. What helps those who keep these fish in their tanks or aquariums is that they stay close to their host and therefore the aggressive behaviour is restricted to that area.

Contrary to popular belief, fish do have personalities. With Clownfish there are very aggressive, moderately aggressive, mild-mannered and even shy and easily startled species. This must be kept in mind when selecting and combining fish in a tank. For example, a shy Skunk Clownfish might be bullied or attacked by more aggressive tank mates.

2) Compatibility with other fish species and marine life

While Clownfish are aggressive when it comes to defending their host, they are certainly not amongst the more aggressive fish that one encounters in tanks and aquariums. Clownfish are fairly small and they don't move quickly either. This makes them vulnerable to carnivorous and larger fish. This must be kept in mind when selecting fish for a tank.

Fish that are a good combination with Clownfish include the following species:

- ✓ Angelfish
- ✓ Blennies
- ✓ Gobies
- ✓ Anglers
- ✓ Dottybacks
- ✓ Tangs

- ✓ Dartfish
- ✓ Wrasses
- ✓ Hawkfish
- ✓ Cardinalfish
- ✓ Damselfish
- ✓ Puffers
- ✓ Gammas.

They can also be placed with a range of marine invertebrates such as sponges, marine worms, star fish, sea cucumbers, small crustaceans such as shrimp, sea urchins and, of course, sea anemones as long as it is a species that is compatible with the specific Clownfish species.

One can also add "live rocks" and various types of hard and soft corals. A live rock is one that has been taken out of the sea and then placed into seawater so that it is still home to a range of micro and / or macroscopic marine life that offers benefits to the tank and its occupants.

3) Compatibility with other Clownfish species

Most Clownfish species don't usually get on well with other Clownfish. Although the less aggressive species can be put together in large tanks, there is still a chance that they will attack each other and fight.

If one does want to put multiple Clownfish together, the tank or aquarium must be large and it's a good idea to place them all in the tank at the same time rather than over time. If there is already a fish in the tank and one wants a second one, one should get a smaller fish that is a juvenile or a male.

Putting different species of Clownfish together is rarely successful. However, as previously stated, if the tank is very large one can be lucky and the fish co-exist fairly peaceably.

4) *What species the Clownfish is incompatible with*

Generally speaking Clownfish get on well with most other fish and with invertebrates including shrimp. However, they are incompatible with:

- Other species of Clownfish
- Snappers
- Groupers
- Eels
- Anglers
- Triggerfish
- Lionfish.

In other words, don't' combine Clownfish with larger, predatory fish or other Clownfish species. Different species of Clowns will fight with each other.

Most species of Clownfish are fine in a pair in a tank. However, they may not even want to share their aquarium with another pair or individuals of the same species as them!

5) *Bullying of new tank inhabitants*

It is not unusual for new arrivals to be chased or even attacked by the fish that are already in residence. As previously indicated, many Clownfish species are territorial and will want to show the newcomer where he is not welcome! If this bullying is of concern, there are a few tricks one can try.

The first option is to partition off a section of your aquarium or tank so that you keep the aggressive fish away from the others. You can use any type of barrier that is easy to clean, won't contaminate the water and allows water to pass freely through it. For example, one can use a plastic grid like that used for lighting systems or some kind of plastic mesh.

A plastic vegetable or pasta strainer or colander would also work. One simply floats it in the tank and it acts as a holding area for the aggressive fish, which one catches in a net and places in the receptacle. Leave the problematic fish in its temporary 'cage' for around 4 hours, by which time it should be safe to reintroduce it into the tank because the new tank inhabitant or inhabitants will have had a chance to adjust and settle in by then.

Both of these options are both inexpensive and easy to manage. Using one or both will greatly reduce the stress experienced by tank inmates and the chances of injury.

Chapter 4: Buying your Clownfish

1) Wild caught versus a Clownfish bred in captivity

The general consensus is that Clownfish bred in captivity offer advantages over one that has been caught in the wild.

> ➤ Captive-bred fish are far less likely to carry disease or parasites. Wild-caught specimens, on the other hand, often carry parasites of various kinds. Diseases and internal or external parasites threaten the fish's health and can also be passed on to other fish in the tank.

> ➤ They are used to people and are even 'pleased' to see people approach the tank because they associate them with food. Fish that are captured in the wild are invariably shy and often frightened. This usually passes with time but wild-caught fish are never quite as relaxed around people.

> ➤ Captive-bred fish acclimatize to tank life far more easily. Although moving to a new tank is stressful, is it far less so for these fish than for those taken from the open oceans and placed in a tank.

> In addition, captive-bred fish are used to small spaces, sharing tank space with other fish and species and with artificial fish food. Even so, correct acclimation procedures are essential with any fish, and they will be discussed in detail in a later chapter.

> ➤ "Shipping stress" is caused by one or more of the changes and moves that a fish would go through. These include collection, exportation/shipment, importation, placed in a new tank at a wholesaler, transported, rehoused in another tank at a retailer and then moved again once it has been bought by an aquarist who takes it home.

Captive-bred fish do not go through several of these traumatic changes. Fish bought from online retailers usually miss out yet another of these stressful changes.

➤ Clownfish captured in the wild are far more likely to exhibit aggressive behaviour, as they will be more territorial than captive-bred fish. In the wild, these fish must defend their territory and hosts and they will continue to act in this way once in captivity. This can lead to injuries or even deaths if they are placed in tanks with other less aggressive fish.

Captive bred fish don't have this history of fighting to defend their host and to survive. This is due to the fact that they seldom have an anemone host and therefore are not aggressively territorial.

➤ With captive-bred or tank reared fish one is far more likely to get a young fish as most are sold when they are less than a year old. There is no way of assessing the age of a wild-caught Clownfish and one could get a fish that is already approaching the end of its lifespan.

➤ There is mortality with both captive and wild Clownfish but this can and should be reduced by ensuring that tank conditions are optimal and by reducing the stress the fish experiences. Mortality due to disease and parasites can be hard to avoid.

The mortality rate with wild caught fish is, not surprisingly, higher than with tank reared fish. As already discussed, these fish are subjected to far more handling and stress and have to make huge adjustments to life in a tank. They also may already be fairly old.

Furthermore, both captive-bred and wild caught fish will die if they are introduced into a tank without correct acclimation and into a tank environment that is not correct for them. Those who buy these and any other fish or pet have a responsibility to give it the correct care and environment.

➢ One area in which captive-bred Clownfish have been criticized is in relation to their markings (stripes) and colouring. Some specimens can be dull but often colours deepen and intensify once the fish is settled in an ideal tank environment and when well fed.

There are also some fish that have broken or incomplete stripes or atypical markings of some sort. It is quite possible that these natural variations occur in the wild too. However, these unusual Clownfish may not survive long in the oceans.

➢ At this stage, captive-bred or tank raised Clownfish are more expensive but only fairly marginally so. The advantages that these fish offer aquarists over wild-caught specimens are thought to more than make up for the price difference. Some fish breeders also believe that as technology and other relevant factors improve, captive-bred fish will at some point cost less than their wild-caught counterparts.

2) Male and female Clownfish

When a Clownfish hatches it is sexually immature. In other words, it is neither male nor female. Most hatchlings become male as they begin to mature. However, there are some individuals that stay sexually immature all their life because of environmental factors.

There are environmental factors that need to be present before a Clownfish will change sex:

• The fish must be between 12 and 24 months old and therefore physically mature

• It will become male if there is a dominant female in the environment and no male

• It will become female if there is no female in the environment

- A fish will remain sexless if there is already a dominant male and female pair in the area.

Other situations will also impact on the sex of the fish and the hierarchy of a group of Clownfish:

- In a group, hierarchy is based on dominance and the most dominant fish will become female. The second most dominant will become a male and the female's mate. The rest of the group will remain sexually immature but they will have a hierarchy of their own.

- If the female dies or is removed from the school the dominant male will change sex and become the dominant female. The second most dominant but sexually immature fish will then become a male.

A sexually mature Clownfish that attempts to join an existing group is unlikely to succeed. In most cases, it will be driven away or even killed. However, if the intruder is strong and aggressive enough it may kill or drive away the female or dominant male and then replace that fish it killed.

How one can tell of a fish is male or female

It is extremely hard, and sometimes completely impossible, to tell whether a fish is male or female. There are a few ways one can establish gender with some species of Clownfish:

- ✓ *Size*: The complication with this feature is that male versus female size is species specific. For example, with Wide Band Clownfish the male and female are the same size but with Maroon Clownfish the males are approximately half the size of the females. The Clarkii complex of fish, on the other hand, is characterised by a minimal difference in size, with the females only slightly larger than the males.

- ✓ *Colour*: This can be an indicator of sex but, like size, is not always a reliable one. Male and female Tomato and Maroon Clownfish are brightly coloured but an aging female will get darker in colour. However, Clarkii female fish usually have white tails and males and juveniles have yellow tails.

✓ *Behaviour*: Female Clownfish are more aggressive. The males are submissive and attentive to the females. Male Clownfish may exhibit dramatic submissive behaviour such as making quivering or shaking movements.

So what is the dead give-away and sometimes only sure way to know? If a Clownfish lays eggs it's a female and if it fertilizes the eggs it's a male!

3) How to ensure the Clownfish you want is healthy

While it is not possible to be 100% sure that a Clownfish is free of disease and parasites, there are certain basics that one should check:

- The eyes should be clear and not clouded or opaque
- The fish should be active (swimming with ease, able to change direction etc.)
- Breathing should be easy and not laboured or erratic
- It should have a healthy appetite
- The fish should look clean (no blotches, lumps or cysts, or 'scaly' or white patches)
- The fins should not have ragged edges
- There should be no spots or white patches inside the mouth.

Chapter 5: What you need to buy for your Clownfish

1) Essential basic equipment & supplies

While this is not necessarily an exhaustive list, it does give an indication of the basic items or supplies required in order to set up a tank or aquarium for Clownfish.

- Tank or aquarium of an appropriate size
- Cover for the aquarium or tank
- Substrate for the bottom of the tank or aquarium
- Décor (live rocks, coral etc.)
- Algae sheets or attack pad
- Filter
- Thermometer
- Air-stone
- Air pump
- Heater
- Full spectrum light
- Water conditioner
- Hydrometer or refractometer
- Aquarium salt
- Water test kit
- Suitably sized net
- Protein skimmer
- Appropriate food.

Investing in a book or two about marine aquariums generally and / or Clownfish specifically is also recommended.

2) The aquarium or tank

It is suggested that the small to medium sized species of Clownfish need an aquarium that holds a minimum of 20 gallons or 91 litres (UK) or 76 litres (US). Larger species will require a tank or aquarium that holds 30 gallons or 136 litres (UK) or 113.5

5) *Lighting and items to combat algae to the tank*

Once you have cured the live rocks and run the tank or aquarium to make sure that the temperature and salinity levels are correct and constant, the next step is to test to establish that the levels of nitrite and ammonia in the water are as they should be: 0 parts per million.

Now that these elements are on track it is time to add the lighting. Ideally an aquarium or tank lighting system should be placed on a timer so that even if you are not home there will be light for the necessary number of hours each day. Clownfish don't actually require a great deal of light. However, other fish or the invertebrates in the tank or aquarium might. The Clownfish will not be harmed by the extra light.

After light has been introduced to the tank, there will be a significant amount of algae growth or what is known as algae bloom. An aquarist wants to avoid this as it impacts negatively on water quality, the health of the creatures in the aquarium, the way the tank looks, visibility and workload for you, as you will have to clean the tank.

The way to avoid algae bloom is by using what is called an algae attack pack. These packs are a natural way of controlling algae growth and maintaining clear, good quality water. An algae attack pack does not contain chemicals, minerals or any artificial substances. Depending on the type of pack you buy you will be introducing any or all of the following into your marine aquarium:

- Hermit Crabs of various types
- Different kinds of marine snails
- Abalone.

Some of these or specific species of them can't be legally kept in some countries so make sure you check before investing in one of these packs.

The algae attack pack is simply added to the aquarium just before the lights are put on for the first time. Each pack gives details of the acclimation or acclimatisation process required. The filtration system in your tank will then have to adjust to accommodate the new residents of your aquarium. The live rock or rocks will help with this process too.

When the algae pack snails and / or crabs have been in the tank for a few days, you need to test the water again, focussing on nitrite and ammonia levels, as these will be affected by the new arrivals. Once the levels of these two toxins have reached 0 you can begin the exciting process of introducing your Clownfish, other fish and invertebrates!

6) Introducing fish and invertebrates to the aquarium

Before you can take this step you need to go through this checklist:

- ✓ You have cured the live rocks you have used so they are not producing toxins

- ✓ You have arranged the rocks in such as way as to create caves and allow space for swimming and free water flow

- ✓ The nitrite and ammonia levels in the tank are at zero and remain that way

- ✓ The temperature remains correct and constant

- ✓ The salinity levels are correct and constant

- ✓ The lighting and filtration systems are working correctly

- ✓ You have installed an algae attack pack that has acclimated

- ✓ There is no algae bloom

And, importantly:

- ✓ You have done research on the various fish and invertebrate species

- ✓ You have learnt all you can about general marine tank care

✓ You have made sure that the fish you want to place in your aquarium with your Clownfish are compatible!

If you can tick off each of these items, you are ready to begin stocking your tank!

However, there are a few rules that govern this exciting and fun stage of setting up a tank or aquarium:

- It is very important that you introduce stock gradually so that the various filtration systems – mechanical and biological – can adjust to each new batch of inhabitants.

- Begin with the fish and other species that are docile and non-aggressive or territorial. They need a chance to settle and establish themselves before the arrival of the more assertive species. It is suggested that they should be left in the tank for several weeks before larger or more aggressive species are introduced.

In terms of how many fish one can have in a tank or aquarium, there is a guideline rather than a hard and fast rule because it depends on several factors, including the species involved and their requirements and temperaments. Generally, it is thought that one can have 0.5 inches or 1.25 centimetres of adult or fully-grown fish for every gallon or 3.7 US or 4.5 litres UK of water in the tank.

7) The easiest corals for your tank or aquarium

One can use a number of corals and polyps in a tank or aquarium but not all of them are easy to care for. The least demanding are generally considered to be:

- Mushroom and Toadstool Corals
- Leather Corals
- Sea Mat and Button Polyps
- Star, Green Star and Daisy Polyps
- Finger Leather and Colt Corals
- Fox, Jasmine and Ridge Corals

- Moon, Pineapple and Star Corals
- Honeycomb, Wreath, Moon and Star Corals
- Zoanthid Corals
- Lobed, Open and Flat Brain Corals
- Closed and Dented Brain Corals.

These various coral and polyp species are found in an astounding array of shapes, textures and sizes. Their colours range from muted greens to vibrant pinks, reds and blues. As a result, they add great visual appeal to an aquarium. They also perform important functions for the tank as a whole and for its occupants.

8) Waste management: a detritus attack pack

The final stage of tank or aquarium set-up is the addition of a detritus attack pack that contains those invertebrates that help to maintain the water parameters at healthy levels. The size of the pack you will need will be determined by the size of your tank.

These packs contain invertebrates such as certain species of starfish, conches, shrimp and snails. What these creatures have in common is that they feed on the waste and food left by the other tank inhabitants. Without these invertebrates, waste matter will accumulate in the tank, encourage algae growth and have a very negative impact on the quality of the water.

9) More on live rocks and live sand

Although live rocks have been discussed, they are such amazing things, and perform so many essential functions, that they deserve more attention. The benefits of live rocks include:

o   Providing a base on which corals and sponges can grow

o   Acting as an extremely efficient biological filter that deals with waste and nitrites

o   Playing a large role in keeping the pH levels of the water within the correct parameters by releasing calcium carbonate o   Providing a home and refuge for various species of fish and invertebrates and for desirable bacteria that help with nitrification

o   Adding visual appeal and interest to the tank or aquarium.

Live sand is also an effective filter and the organisms in it help to keep the water clear.

10) Air and water flow systems

The majority of the oxygen that is in tank or aquarium water is dissolved oxygen from the surface of the water. The water works the same way our bodies do because oxygen is taken in and carbon dioxide and other toxic or unwanted gasses are released.

While the water surface does take care of much of the oxygen that the creatures in your tank will need, you will still need to get some kind of air system. There is a wide range of these devices available currently and you will need to select one based on the size of your aquarium or tank, the fish and so forth in it and your budget. It's a good idea to get advice from a reliable and honest dealer ,as it can become confusing.

The main types of air systems one can get are:

- Under-gravel bubble systems
- Air stones.

Both are driven by electrical air pumps. In terms of water flow or circulation, aquarists often use a combination of:

- Powerheads
- Wave-makers and oscillators.

Under-gravel filters

As the name suggests, these fairly thin and flat filters are placed under the gravel or sand at the bottom of a tank or aquarium when you are setting it up. While they are actually there to aid with filtration and water quality, they also release air bubbles, which move the water up to the surface. This helps with the exchange of various gasses into and out of the water.

Other advantages of these filters are that the bubbles that are released are attractive and these items of equipment are relatively inexpensive.

On the down side, some tank owners find the constant sound made by the bubbles irritating. Others find it soothing…

Air stones

Air stones are very popular with a lot of aquarists. One can either buy or even make an air stone. The name is a little deceptive in that these items are not necessarily stone. They could be made of wood, glass or ceramic. They are connected to a hose through which air generated by an air pump.

Although they are aesthetically appealing, are inexpensive, release air bubbles that move water up to the surface and so enable the exchange of gasses, there are disadvantages too.

The primary disadvantage of air stones is that they are not able to move a large volume of water quickly because they simply don't have the power. This means they are not very efficient and are totally inadequate for larger tanks.

The water in an aquarium should ideally move both horizontally and upwards or vertically. This ensures that all the water in the tank is properly circulated. Air stones can't achieve this either.

Other problems and drawbacks include:

- The air flow can be irregular and the air pressure is often too low because the pump is inadequate for the size or depth of the tank or the pipe is too long

- They clog up and the air flow diminishes further or even stops

- The pipe running to the stone can become squashed or bent and this will also negatively affect or even stop air flow

- They need to be replaced much more often than other types as they become worn out or blocked

- They create fine salt spray, which builds up in the tank and can lead to problems such as salt creep (more on what salt creep is and how to deal with it later)

However, they are an important part of protein skimming or foam fractionating in a tank (more on this later).

Powerheads

A Powerhead is an electrical unit that can be safely submerged in water. This is thanks to the fact that they are sealed. They can be positioned on the bottom of a tank or attached to the sides. While Powerheads are used to run or power various pieces of equipment in an aquarium such as various types of filters, protein skimmers and air pumps, they are also ideal for water circulation. Naturally, the larger the tank, the more Powerheads one must use.

The basic advantages they offer an aquarist are that they are very effective, economical in terms of power consumption and they are fairly inexpensive. They make the tank a healthier environment for all the inhabitants because of the strength and consistency of the water flow they generate. The associated benefits include:

- Greatly improved water quality

- Improved oxygenation, which promotes the health of the tank's occupants

- Reduced detritus in the tank by improving filtration

- Algae growth is deterred or significantly reduced

- Food brought to stationary creatures in the tank

- The tank inhabitants are stimulated to move and so get exercise, which improves their health.

All of these are due to one factor: the strong water circulation throughout the tank or aquarium generated by Powerheads.

While there is no doubt that buying a Powerhead is an excellent investment, it is also necessary to place them with care and caution. For instance, some anemones and corals thrive in a strong current while others will not flourish at all. This means the Powerhead must be placed where it will not adversely affect anything in the tank.

As there is a confusing array of Powerheads on the market, here are some tips to guide you in terms of choosing a suitable and reliable Powerhead for your aquarium or tank:

✓ Spend a little more money to buy a brand name Powerhead such as one manufactured by Hagen or Marineland for example. If you do so, you can rest assured that you are getting a reliable product that is tested and should last. 'Budget' versions may cost less initially but they are far more likely to burn out.

✓ You need to invest in a Powerhead that you can get parts for easily if you need them. It also helps if the unit can be opened and disassembled and then reassembled easily for repair purposes.

✓ The interior may need cleaning from time to time and this is another reason why it should be a unit that can be opened with ease. If you can't clean the interior regularly or as necessary, it may burn out if it becomes clogged.

✓ A good Powerhead will be moisture proof and, preferably, epoxy sealed. This will prevent both water getting in and electricity leaking out!

✓ Buy a model that has a screen of some kind that will prevent any of the fish or invertebrates in your tank accidentally being sucked into the intake hole of the Powerhead. Just make sure the holes in the screen are not too small because they will clog up with dirt very quickly. This in turn will reduce the water intake, which can lead to the motor becoming overheated or even burning out.

✓ The model you buy must also be saltwater safe if you are placing it into a marine or saltwater aquarium. Not all Powerheads are able to cope with saltwater.

✓ If possible, select a Powerhead that allows you to adjust the water rate. This will mean that you can reduce or increase the rate of flow (or even reverse it) it depending on the needs of your tank and its inhabitants.

✓ As an optional extra you could purchase a directional flow diffuser that fits onto the Powerhead. This will enable you to direct the water flow in your tank with even greater accuracy and care.

Once you have selected the model you want, you need to decide how many Powerheads you need and where you will place it or them in your tank. The size of your aquarium is the most significant factor.

If you have a tank that is 20 gallons (91 litres UK or 76 litres US) or less you have two options: a single, large Powerhead or two less powerful ones that can be placed at either end of the tank. Medium to large tanks will need more units and more powerful ones. Often a smaller unit is placed at each corner.

The bottom line is that you need as many Powerheads as it will take to create the amount of water circulation or flow that your tank requires in order to maintain good water quality.

The final important aspect of Powerheads is flow rates. These will also depend on whether you have a tank that only contains fish or a reef tank as one would have with Clownfish. Most experienced hobbyists believe that the water in the tank should be turned over, or circulated throughout the tank, between 6 and 10 times an hour. A few aquarists say that reef tanks should have a flow of 15 to 20 times an hour.

What is essential is that a balance is struck between:

- Circulating the water

- Not making fish swim against currents constantly as this will exhaust them, or creating such strong and constant currents that invertebrates are damaged or harmed.

Wave makers and Oscillators

Wave makers are connected to controlling devices that turn the Powerheads on and off at set and regular intervals. This creates a variable current and waves. Oscillators, on the other hand, create random currents by rotating the Powerhead rather than turning it on and off.

11) Protein Skimmers

In this context "protein" refers to the muck that floats around in the water. It consists of bits of uneaten food and waste matter of various kinds. This must be removed from the water and this is achieved through skimming or, to use the correct technical term, the process of "foam fractionating".

This sounds complicated and impressive but it isn't. Skimming is quite simply using water bubbles to remove protein molecules from the water.

What happens is that as the column or columns of air bubbles rise from the floor of the tank or aquarium, the molecules of protein attach themselves to the surface of the bubbles. These waste products rise to the surface of the water, where they are collected in a container.

The trick to successful skimming is that there must be a large number of bubbles because the more bubbles there are, the more protein will be collected. In addition, the longer the bubble column is the better as this gives the bubbles more time to attract protein molecules to them. Furthermore, the smaller the bubble the more slowly it rises and the more effectively it gathers protein molecules. In summary, bubble columns should:

✓ Contain a lot of bubbles
✓ Be as long as possible
✓ Consist of small bubbles or at least some small bubbles.

There are two types of skimming apparatus: co-current and counter-current.

One can have a vertical column of bubbles. These bubbles follow their natural tendency to rise to the surface. When they reach the surface of the water they burst and leave the proteins behind, often in the form of foam. Skimmers like this that use vertical bubble columns are known as co-current skimmers.

Other skimmers, called counter-current skimmers, force the bubbles downward through the water or even sideways. Again, this is in order to keep the bubbles in the water for as long as possible so that they collect the optimal amount of protein.

In either even the air that is used to create the bubbles is usually sent into the skimmer by means of a diffuser such as an air stone or an air pump.

What to Look For in a Protein Skimmer

As with other pieces of tank equipment, there is a wide range of skimmers from which to choose. There are some things that you should look for in a protein skimmer or a foam fractionating system:

- Look for a skimmer that is easy to maintain. You don't want a model that is difficult to work with so that you battle to remove, for instance, the collection container.

- The skimmer should be adjustable so that you can change and manage the water flow in the skimmer's reaction chamber. A manufacturer's claim that "no adjustments are needed" often actually translates as "no adjustments are possible"!

- You need to know where you are going to put the skimmer in your tank or aquarium. That will help you decide which model to get as some, for instance, are placed in the tank and others on it.

As with any aspect of a tank or aquarium's equipment, don't ever be reluctant or afraid to ask for information and advice!

12) Heating/Temperature control

Clownfish, like all fish, are cold blooded. This is also true of their invertebrate tank-mates. This means that they are not able, as we are, to raise and lower their body temperature in response to the environment. It is therefore the tank owner's responsibility to provide heat and maintain the correct temperature for the creatures in the aquarium.

The required temperature or the temperature range depends on the species of marine animal you have in your tank. The fact that most marine creatures can't survive temperature fluctuations of more than a few degrees makes it essential that you find out about the range for each species and make sure they are compatible. For example, for Clownfish the water temperature must be between 75 and 82° Fahrenheit or 24 and 28° Celsius.

Types of heating units

As with all the other items for your tank you will be faced with a choice when it comes to buying a heater for it. There are three options:

- *Heating cable systems*: These are placed under the substrate of the tank and are connected to an electronic controlling unit. While these systems are more often used for fresh water tanks, some marine or saltwater aquarists do use them.

  The primary advantage of cable heating systems is that they distribute heat very evenly throughout the tank. This is mainly due to the fact that heat rises.

However, there is a major drawback with them, especially for those who have a reef tank for their Clownfish. If the system goes wrong and must be repaired or replaced, you will have to remove everything from the tank before you can remove it from under the substrate!

- *Submersible heaters*: These heaters can be mounted from the side of a tank or placed on the substrate. Because they are fully submerged in the water, they heat the water very effectively. They are also easy to lift out if necessary.

- *Hang-on-tank heaters*: These, as the name implies, hang on the interior of the tank. They are only partly submerged beneath the water line. While they, too, are easy to remove if needs be, they are not efficient heaters because they are not fully submerged.

Words of caution

If you opt for either a submersible or a hang-on heater, it is a good idea to have more than one so you have one in reserve. This way if the heater malfunctions or breaks down, you have a backup unit available. Sometimes one doesn't have time to get a new one before the temperature in the tank changes significantly…with lethal results.

If you have a medium or large aquarium, you will need more than one heater anyway in order to maintain constant temperatures throughout the tank. In this situation, you should also have a heating unit in reserve.

Regardless of which type of system you select, remember to make sure that it can be used in saltwater and is not only suitable for fresh water.

Other factors to consider

When selecting and installing a heating unit or units you need to keep in mind that it or they won't be the only source of heat. Some heat will be given off by lights, other tank equipment such as Powerheads, heating sources in the room such as vents or central heating units and even the seasonal temperature extremes in your area that make a difference to the ambient temperature in the room.

All of these heat sources and temperature factors will affect the temperature in the tank. This in turn will impact on your decision about the size heater your aquarium will need.

Fortunately, there is a rule of thumb guideline used by aquarists that will be of help: you need to use 2.5 – 5 watts per gallon (3.75 US or 4.55 UK litres) of water. Once you have calculated how many watts your tank will need you can work out the size heater and the number you will need.

How to deal with an overheating crisis

The inhabitants of a tank or aquarium are very susceptible to changes in water temperature. Water that becomes too warm is fatal even faster than water that has become too cool. Tank owners who battle the most with this are those in very hot climates. However, it can affect other aquarists too.

Regardless of the reason for it, an overheating problem must be resolved as fast as possible. There are things that can be done quickly and without special equipment:

- *Open or remove covers or hoods*: A cover or hood on a tank or aquarium traps heat. If the cover on your tank is hinged, you need to open it and leave it open until the crisis has passed. If there is a lid on your aquarium, you need to remove it and leave it off for as long as necessary. (Consider not putting it back because using a hood or cover is not generally recommended because they reduce aeration, lower oxygen levels and increase carbon dioxide levels).

- *Fans*: Place small fans near the tank or clip-on fans on the sides or top of the tank. The fans should be directed in such a way that the air flows across the top of the water. The flow of air should be strong but not so much so that it causes any significant surface disturbance.

o *Adjust the lighting in the tank*: As mentioned earlier, lights generate heat in addition to illumination. Different types of lighting give off varying amounts of heat. Fluorescent lights produce the least amount of heat and metal halides the most. An easy way to reduce heat, therefore, is to have 'hot' lights on for fewer hours each day or, alternatively, only have the fluorescents on. You could do this for up to 2 days without impacting negatively on the tank's inhabitants.

o *Use ice*: This is also not a complex solution but it is both effective and quick. It's a good idea to keep a few ice packs in the freezer in case they are needed…You need to begin by removing some of the water from your tank because the water level will rise when you introduce the ice. You can use plastic bottles that you filled with water and froze or sealed bags that contain ice cubes. Either type can be placed into the tank where they will float.

o *Buy or make a chiller*: You can buy a chiller from a retailer if you wish to do so. More practical aquarists make their own chillers using ice, an ice chest, a water pump and plastic tubes. There are a number of plans and ideas for DIY chillers available on the Internet.

With any and all of these methods it is essential to monitor the temperature regularly. The last thing one wants is for the water to go from too hot to too cold! In order to monitor it accurately, you will require an accurate thermometer of some kind.

13) Thermometers

As with other pieces of equipment, thermometers are no different in that the aquarist is spoiled for choice. You can get one that gives readings in either Fahrenheit or Celsius or both. While there are many kinds of thermometer, they all do the same job. This can make selecting one harder. What is helpful is to look at the pros and cons of each type.

▪ *Floating thermometers*: This is perhaps the most widely known and earliest kind. They are inexpensive, easy to read, compact, and can either be left to float around or be attached to the side by means of a plastic suction cup.

The downside is that the suction cups wear out and must be replaced regularly or are not effective and don't adhere properly, if the thermometer is free floating it can bang into the glass sides of the tank and break as these thermometers are also made of glass, the numbering is small and can be hard to read and if it is floating one has to look for it each time.

- *Magnetic thermometers*: These thermometers offer a great deal. They are easy to attach: the thermometer is positioned against the glass on the inside of the tank and the magnet is placed outside the tank. They are held firmly in place, have easy to read numbers, a broad temperature range and don't corrode.

The only disadvantage is the white plastic casing is not attractive and makes these thermometers highly visible.

- *Stainless steel thermometers*: These, too, are inexpensive types of thermometer and they are usually just mounted to the edge of the tank. Because they are made of stainless steel, they don't corrode or rust. They are easier to read than the smaller glass thermometers.

However, because they are fairly large and shiny, they can look unattractive. They also sink if they are dropped or knocked off the aquarium rim.

- *Standing thermometers*: These are compact, affordable and easy to read. They are weighted so they sink to the bottom but remain vertical. However, they come with a host of drawbacks.

They have a tendency to move around in the currents and can bang against hard surfaces such as rocks or the sides of the aquarium. This makes these thermometers susceptible to breakage. They can also be hard to spot because they move and hard to read as they may be behind or against something.

- *Stick-on Liquid Crystal Display (LCD) thermometers*: These are the easiest thermometer type to install as you just peel off the backing and stick it onto the outside of the tank. Other advantages are that they are low cost, available in a range of sizes and various temperature ranges.

  However, the lamination may separate over time and they can be difficult to read.

- *Remote Sensor Digital thermometers*: Hardly surprisingly, these thermometers are not as inexpensive as others, but they are still not too costly. The advantages include their compact size, the fact that they are easy to read and that the LED display is placed on the outside of the tank or near the tank. A sensor cord runs from the display into the water and this is part of why these thermometers also have disadvantages.

  The LCD is attached by means of suction cups, which are not always effective and will need replacing. The length of the sensor cord dictates where the LCD can be placed. In addition the batteries that power the thermometer will need periodic replacing.

- *Submersible LCD digital thermometers*: This kind of thermometer has a great deal in their favour: they are compact, are fixed in place, have an easy to read LCD display and they are wireless and fully submersible.

  They are attached by means of suction cups, which can be problematic and will need to be replaced, as will the batteries that power the thermometer. Not all of these types of LCD thermometer arte suitable for saltwater aquariums so one needs to check on that.

- *Temperature Alert Remote Sensor digital thermometers*: These thermometers cost a little more than most others but they are compact and easy to read thanks to the LED display. The biggest selling point is the fact that these thermometers include automatic temperature setting high/low alarms which can be extremely useful.

The length of the sensor cord will limit where the LCD can be placed and the cord is visible. The batteries will of course require periodic replacing. These thermometers are made in either Fahrenheit or Celsius so you need to check that before buying one.

If you feel confused or simply overwhelmed by the range of types of thermometer available, you can find more information and advice online or from a retailer who is familiar with aquariums and the equipment that is necessary for them.

14) UV Sterilisers

An Ultraviolet or UV Steriliser is used to stop free-floating microorganisms from spreading in a tank or aquarium. This in turn serves to control infections and cross-infections between fish, invertebrates and corals. It does so by using UV light to kill these free-floating microorganisms. They have no effect on microorganisms etc. that are already in or on marine creatures. What is essential is that the UV steriliser is installed and operated correctly.

These sterilisers work by exposing the water that flows through them to UV light from their bulbs. The wavelength of the light is about 254 nanometres or 2537 Angstroms and this irradiates the water as it passes through the steriliser. The effect on bacteria and algae is to mutate its DNA, which in turn prevents them from multiplying or growing.

These sterilisers, if properly used, are said to be effective against algae, bacteria, parasitic protozoa and viruses. The larger the organism is the higher the required dose of UV will be. For instance, algae must be exposed to far higher doses than a virus has to be.

A UV Steriliser will produce different amounts of light depending on the wattage of the bulb: the higher the wattage, the more UV light. It's important to remember, though, that these bulbs degrade with age and must be replaced every 6 months or so.

There are several factors that impact on the effectiveness of a UV Steriliser that should be kept in mind:

- UV light is far less effective at sterilizing water that is murky or dirty. The UV Steriliser must therefore be placed after the filters so that the water is as clear as it can be.

- The UV lamp must be kept clean because if it becomes covered by a film or layer of deposits of some sort it will not give off as much UV as possible.

- UV can only penetrate 5mm (a mere 13/64") into salt water. This means that the lamp must be very close to the water.

- Not surprisingly, the longer water is exposed to UV the more microorganisms will be killed. The length of time the water is exposed is determined by the flow rate: the slower the flow the longer the exposure. Using a long bulb will also increase the exposure period.

- Temperature is a further variable that plays a role because UV is optimally produced in warmer temperatures (104 to 110° Fahrenheit or 40 to 43° Celsius). Using a sleeve around the bulb can help to insulate the bulb against the colder water in a saltwater or reef aquarium.

While a UV Steriliser certainly offers very significant benefits, they do have a downside:

- They are of no use against any of the disease-causing microorganisms that are not free swimming and against string algae.

- UV can also destroy beneficial bacteria that live in substances such as substrate.

- UV light can destroy the properties of some medications that are in the water. In order to prevent this "denaturing" of medication the UV should be switched off until the treatment is completed.

- They can cause a rise in water temperature and a chiller may have to be used to counteract this.

It is also important to keep in mind that they don't replace filters and good water quality parameter controls. UV is a nice-to-have extra form of protection.

Chapter 7: Water and other parameters

1) Salinity and pH levels

Salinity

Salinity refers to the levels of dissolved salt in water. In a marine tank that is home to Clownfish, the salinity levels should range from 1.020 to 1.026 grams per kilogram or 0.0359 to 0.0361 ounces.

As with other parameters, you need to check them for all the species in your tank so that they are all happy and healthy.

Acidity/alkalinity (pH)

Maintaining the correct pH level is a very important part of caring for a tank and keeping fish healthy. Power of Hydrogen, or pH, is the measure that tells one if something is acidic or alkaline. A pH reading of 7 is the neutral border between the two. Readings below 7 indicate acidity and those above 7 are alkaline.

Acids can be caused by several things in a tank or aquarium: acids created by waste in the tank that is not effectively removed by filtration and protein skimming, too much carbon dioxide (CO_2) because of poor water circulation and gas exchanges and, finally, nitric acid released by biological filters such as live rocks. All of these build up in the water and drop the pH level dangerously if they are not dealt with.

The oceans and seas have a way of combating all of these acids: they contain what are called "buffers". These consist of various chemicals including hydroxide, calcium, carbonate, bicarbonate and borate. They slow down the drop in pH levels. In order to deal effectively with acidity in a tank an aquarist must make use of the same buffers.

Ways to avoid pH problems in your tank

The best way to avoid pH problems is to do regular partial water changes - which restore the buffers - and to make sure the tank stays free of the factors that release acids into the water.

One can also invest in a piece of equipment simply called a "doser". This item will automatically introduce a range of supplements and trace elements, including buffers, into the water.

Calcium reactors are also an option to deal with severe or frequent problems with pH levels. They are costly, though.

Ways to combat pH problems in your tank

If you already have a pH problem in your tank, you need to deal with it very fast and effectively or you run the risk of losing your tank's inhabitants. The most common options are:

- ✓ If the pH is too low, you can add either a pH increaser that you can buy at a retailer or you can add bicarbonate of soda, also known as baking soda.

- ✓ If the pH is too high, home remedies to reduce it include adding small amounts of lemon juice or vinegar to the water. Alternatively, you could buy a commercial pH reduction product.

Many aquarists believe that the three most important aspects are water temperature, pH levels and water quality. Although tanks that only house fish can have a wider pH range, reef tanks such as the ones Clownfish require must have a constant pH level to survive. A pH of 8.0 to 8.4 is necessary in reef tanks.

2) Phosphate and Calcium

Phosphate (PO4)

Phosphate (PO4) is a compound of Phosphorous (P), which is a trace element that is found naturally in seawater and is essential for marine and reef aquariums. In the ocean the levels of PO4 is 0.07 parts per million (ppm).

The reason why phosphate levels are of such concern to aquarists is because these compounds are the main source of food or nutrition for various types of algae. So, if there are too many phosphates in a tank there will be significant algae blooms.

Brown algae grow on coral and this has two effects. Firstly, the algae growth dulls and obscures the colours in the coral, causing it to go brown. The covering of algae also results in the coral being unable to absorb the calcium it needs to grow its skeleton.

Phosphates are caused by several factors but the most common ones are the use of unfiltered tap water in the tank either as top-up water or to make up sea salt mixes and substances put into the tank such as foods, activated carbon and even some salt mixes.

For this reason it is strongly suggested that you check ingredient lists on all products so you make sure you are not introducing phosphates or other unwanted compounds or trace elements such as nitrates, for example.

In a reef tank or aquarium, the Phosphate range should be 0.05 to 0.1 ppm. Since a minute quantity such as this is very difficult to access you will need to invest in a reliable and accurate test kit. Various reputable websites recommend test kits manufacturer by LaMotte and Hach. However, your local retailer will be able to offer advice and suggestions.

What one does need to remember is that, while the range might look miniscule, it is vital not to let the levels of Phosphate in a tank get too high. There are several things you can do to prevent phosphate build-up and to correct the level if it gets too high.

The first preventative measure is regular tank maintenance. If you perform regular water changes with good quality water you will go a long way to controlling unwanted trace elements and compounds such as phosphates and nitrates. Routine and frequent tests are also necessary because one can't assume that these elements are controlled thanks to the water changes.

If the phosphate levels in your aquarium are too high you can:

✓ Use commercial and easily available products that are designed to remove phosphates from tanks and aquariums. There is a range of these products on the market.

No matter which product one uses it is essential that they are changed and replenished regularly. If they aren't, they will become saturated with the compounds they have absorbed and will no longer work.

✓ Phosphate levels are also reduced if you add a limewater or *kalkwasser* (KW) solution to the water. Limewater is essentially a diluted form of calcium hydroxide, which is believed to effectively remove phosphate because it contains very high levels of calcium.

✓ The Vodka Method also removes phosphates (and nitrates) but only when used with a protein skimmer. As the name implies, one adds a small amount of Vodka, or ethanol, to the tank water.

Calcium (Ca)

Without calcium in the water in which they live, many molluscs, crustaceans and corals simply can't grow and survive. These life forms extract calcium from the water and use calcium carbonate to build their skeletal structures. There is a complication, though: even if there is calcium in the water it can't be used if the pH is not as it should be.

If both calcium and alkalinity levels in the water are low, calcareous life forms such as those mentioned will not grow or thrive and will die. Calcium, carbonate and pH and alkalinity are interconnected in marine water.

The ideal calcium level in a tank is considered to be about 0.014 ounces per 33.8 fluid ounces US or 35.2 fluid ounces UK or 400 milligrams per litre. This level is slightly higher than those found naturally in the oceans. In order to introduce the required calcium into tank water you will need to use limewater or *kalkwasser*.

In addition to the fact that KW reduces phosphates, it also replaces the calcium that is absorbed and used by the organisms in your aquarium. The amount of limewater you add to the aquarium water will depend on its size and capacity. It will also be affected by the number and type of marine creatures in the tank that require calcium. This means that you may have to make constant adjustments if you introduce new inhabitants or if corals are in a growth phase etc.

Preparing a limewater or KW solution is not difficult but it does require care and safety precautions. The dry powder that is used is caustic and so you don't want to inhale it or have it in contact with your skin. Packets of the dry powder *must* be kept somewhere secure where children and animals can't get to it!

The powder is mixed with distilled or purified water. To this one must add either calcium oxide (CaO) or calcium hydroxide (Ca(HO)2). Some experienced aquarists use calcium chloride instead but this is more complex to prepare and involves additional steps and chemicals. The recipe for the *kalkwasser* for a tank is simple:

i.   Add between 1 teaspoon and 1 tablespoon (most tanks will require 1 rounded teaspoon) of calcium oxide or hydroxide to 1 gallon (3.75 US or 4.55 UK litres) of distilled or purified water. It is suggested that one only make up this quantity at a time.

ii. Mix the power and water carefully and expose it to air for as short a time as possible. If a significant amount of carbon dioxide is absorbed by the mixture, it results in the formation of calcium carbonate and the loss of calcium.

     One knows if this has happened because a white residue forms and settles at the bottom of the container or bottle. Any calcium carbonate must be removed from the solution before it can be used.

iii. Keep the container sealed because each time it is opened carbon dioxide will enter it, form calcium carbonate and destroy useable carbon. This is the main reason why one should prepare small quantities of the solution at a time.

Once you have the KW solution, you need to add it to your tank. However, it can't just be poured in; it must be introduced in a slow and measured way. Here again there are several options.

The first is the use of a commercial or DIY measuring pump or an "auto-doser". These are slow-drip devices much like those used in drips in hospitals. They dispense a controlled amount of solution into the water at set intervals.

The solution is then circulated throughout the tank by the currents generated by Powerheads, oscillators and so forth. The simplest way to introduce the solution is to add it to top-up water and pour this slowly into the aquarium, again letting the current do the in-tank mixing for you.

The most expensive option is to buy and install a calcium reactor. These sophisticated pieces of equipment mix and release the solution for you. They also generate the ideal pH for the mixture and greatly reduce the amount of carbon dioxide that enters the solution so there is no loss of calcium through calcium carbonate formation.

The next option is to purchase calcium supplements that can be introduced into the water. If you use these products, you will avoid the measuring, mixing and adding. The price you pay will be, well, the price you pay for these not inexpensive products.

3) The Vodka treatment

It was very briefly mentioned earlier but this cost-effective remedy to reduce both nitrate and phosphate levels in a tank or aquarium justifies closer inspection. Although there are some aquarists that are very sceptical, others believe that using Vodka is effective. More accurately, one uses alcohol or 95% ethanol rather than Vodka.

Why this method works seems to be due to the fact that alcohol contains inorganic carbon. This type of carbon boosts the growth of bacteria in the water. These bacteria work with the aquarist because they actually incorporate or 'feed' on the phosphates and nitrates in the tank. The bacteria in turn are eaten or absorbed by some tank residents, like many species of sponge, or they are removed when protein skimming occurs.

The Vodka treatment is usually administered each day for three days and involves very small quantities. For example, if you had a 50 gallon tank (189 litres US or 227 litres UK) you would add 5 drops of 80% alcohol per day. This translates to 0.25 millilitres or an insanely small 0.0168 fluid ounces!

Chapter 8: Introducing Clownfish and other creatures into the tank

1) Acclimation

After one has bought Clownfish, other fish and invertebrates one can't just put them into the tank no matter how carefully it has been set up and prepared. Why? All the marine creatures you acquire will have been in water that will have had different pH and salinity levels and temperatures to the water in your aquarium.

Marine animals are *extremely* sensitive to these factors. It is essential that they get used to the changes and differences gradually. This is the purpose of the process called ***acclimation***.

There are a couple of methods one can use. Regardless of which method you opt for, the golden rule with acclimation is not to rush the process. Both methods begin with these steps:

A. Turn off the light or lights in the tank and dim the lights in the room where you will open the box or container the marine creatures are in. Harsh or bright light and sudden exposure to light is very traumatic and will cause stress.

B. Place the still sealed bag in the water in your aquarium. After 15 to 20 minutes the water inside the bag will have slowly adjusted to the temperature of the water in the tank. By keeping the bag sealed you ensure that the level of dissolved oxygen in the water in the bag stays high.

The float method

Once you have completed steps A and B above, and have elected to go with the float method, you need to:

1. Cut the bag open just below the metal clip that seals it. Roll the edge of the bag down about 1 inch or 2.5

centimetres so that you create an air pocket in the rolled up section. This air should be enough to keep the bag afloat.

2. Carefully and slowly add a ½ cup of water from your tank or aquarium to the water in the shipping bag. Continue to add a further ½ cup every 4 or 5 minutes until the shipping bag is full.

3. Remove the bag from the water and drain 50% of the water, being careful not to disturb the occupants of the bag.

4. Float the bag in the aquarium again and repeat step 2 until the bag is full once more.

5. Use a suitable net to carefully catch the marine creature or creatures in the shipping bag and release it/them into the aquarium.

6. Remove the floating shipping bag from the tank and discard the water. It's important that you don't ever place the rest of the water into your tank or aquarium.

The drip method

The drip method is considered to be the preferable one for certain fish and invertebrates such as wrasses, corals, star fish and shrimp. In other words, more sensitive creatures should be acclimatised using this method rather than the float method. The drip method does, however, require additional equipment in the form of air tubing and a bucket or buckets.

The bucket you use must be one that is only used for tank water to prevent possible contamination by, for instance, household cleaning products. Fish should be placed in one bucket and invertebrates in a separate one during acclimation. In addition, the tank owner must be involved throughout the process because progress must be monitored constantly.

The drip method begins with steps A and B as the floating method does. These steps balance the water temperature inside the bag. Once you have achieved this, you need to:

1. Empty the contents of the bag into the bucket. Remember to do this as carefully as possible so as not to stress or injure the marine creatures in them. It's also essential not to expose invertebrates to the air so make sure they stay submerged as you empty the bag.

2. At this stage, the plastic tubing or pipes come into play. You need to run a drip line from your aquarium or tank to the bucket or buckets. It's important to control the flow so that the tube or pipe releases water very slowly. You could buy a control valve or make one by tying a fairly loose knot in the tube or pipe. It's also a good idea to fasten the pipe or tube to something so it stays securely in place.

3. It's not difficult to begin the siphoning process for the drip method. Suck on the end of the pipe or tube until water begins to flow through it from the tank or aquarium. You must then adjust the knot or valve so that the pipe releases only 2 to 4 drips per second.

4. When the amount or volume of water in the bucket has doubled, you need to carefully and slowly discard half of it. Reinsert the tube and double the water volume again.

5. Transfer the fish and/or invertebrates in the bucket(s) to the tank or aquarium. Again, one must be very careful not to expose invertebrates to the air or to touch corals on their fleshier parts.

   If necessary, invertebrates can be scooped out of the bucket in a specimen bag and then the bag should be submerged in the tank. Once the creatures are out of the bag, seal it underwater and remove it from the tank. Be careful not to release too much of the diluted water into the aquarium. The water in the bag and bucket(s) must be discarded.

Specific gravity during acclimation

Furthermore, marine invertebrates and plants are even more sensitive than fish are to changes in specific gravity. Specific gravity, very simply put, provides information about the concentration of solutions such as, for instance, salt water. Invertebrates require a specific gravity of 1.023 to 1.025 or they may become severely traumatised and stressed. Specific gravity must therefore also be carefully monitored during the acclimation process.

In order to test specific gravity one needs to use a suitable tool such as a hydrometer or refractometer. Both measure specific gravity by measuring salinity or salt levels in the water. There is quite a debate about which is better. However, the majority of aquarists seem to feel that the refractometer is far more reliable and easier to use.

Corals and acclimation

There are some species of coral that produce excess mucous or slime during the shipping process. Once the coral has been acclimated, one should hold the coral by the rock or base and shake it gently in the shipping bag before placing it in the tank. One shouldn't be concerned if corals remain closed for the first few days. Once they have adapted and settled they will open.

Some tips and rules with acclimation:

o   Don't rush the acclimation process; be patient.

o   Some fish and invertebrates can appear to have died either before you begin acclimation or during the process. Don't assume it is dead. Continue with acclimation and quite often a marine creature will revive.

o   Don't expose invertebrates to air or handle corals roughly.

o   Don't place an air-stone or introduce air through a pipe or tube into the shipping bag or bucket(s). Doing so increases the pH levels far too quickly and will expose your marine creatures to ammonia, which is lethal for them.

o   Keep the aquarium lights off for at least 4 hours after you introduce new fish and/or invertebrates to the tank or aquarium, as this will help them to adjust more easily to their new environment.

And a final thought...

There is a further stage that could or even should be introduced as part of introducing new stock into a tank or aquarium: the use of a quarantine tank. A quarantine tank, as the name implies, is a separate tank in which new arrivals are kept for two weeks or so before they are introduced into the main tank.

Doing this will greatly reduce the chances that newly arrived fish or invertebrates will introduce parasites or diseases that will infect your existing stock. It also gives the tank owner a chance to monitor the newcomers and make sure they are healthy, adjusting and eating well. It's not as easy to assess these factors once they are in with all the other creatures in the main tank.

Chapter 9: Caring for your Clownfish

1) Basic maintenance

It will be no surprise by now to hear that a saltwater or marine tank is a lot of work. The fact that so many avid aquarists and hobbyists all over the world perform all the tasks that are necessary is proof of how wonderful having a healthy, colourful tank stocked with Clownfish and other fascinating marine creatures is!

What can be very helpful is to draw up a schedule for regular and routine tank maintenance. In addition to feeding the inhabitants of the aquarium, the owner needs to carry out of number of tasks regularly. The basic ones are:

- o Clean out the filter
- o Clean out the container connected to the skimmer
- o Check the various water parameters: temperature, salinity, pH, calcium, phosphate and nitrates
- o Check to ensure that all the equipment is still working
- o Mix up solutions such as saltwater and limewater
- o Replace 25% of the water in the tank
- o Top up the tank
- o Remove any dirt or detritus
- o Monitor the condition of all the fish and invertebrates in the tank.

These tasks are broken down by frequency in more detail later. As a rough guideline, it is recommended by experienced aquarists that one checks:

- Equipment: daily
- Salinity: twice a week
- Temperature: weekly
- Water change: once or twice a month.

Tip: Unplug the heater or heaters before you work on a tank! If you don't, and water levels change in such a way that they impact on the heater, you run the risk of cracking or breaking the glass in the tank or overheating or even burning out the heater.

2) Preparing water for your tank

One can't – or certainly experienced aquarists strongly advise against – just using tap water in an aquarium because it contains substances that are damaging to the water quality and therefore to the creatures living in the tank.

If one needs to top-up a tank, replace some of the water or mix up a solution such as a sea salt mix, one must use treated tap water, bottled water, fresh sea water or distilled water that has not passed through copper pipes during the distillation process.

Why you shouldn't use tap water in an aquarium

The water supplied in towns and cities is put through purification processes. However, this does not mean it is safe to use in a tank. If one does use it, one is likely to encounter problems.

Tap water often contains chlorine and the attendant chloramine bonds. One can use a de-chlorinating product but while they do remove chlorine, they don't usually break the chloramine bonds. You could look for a product, however, that specifically deals with chloramines.

In addition, tap water contains metals and, sometimes, bacteria. There are often heavy metals such as iron and copper in this water. These are often lethal for the fish and other creatures in a tank. The bacteria may be there because some strains will survive the chlorine used to treat the water. Once these bugs are in your aquarium they will have a chance to flourish and infect your precious marine stock.

Furthermore, tap water contains elements and compounds that do belong in water such as silicates, phosphates and nitrates. The problem arises because they often contain high levels or high concentrations of these substances.

As previously discussed, one already has to deal with some of these compounds when they are generated by marine creatures in the tank. Adding more causes headaches for the tank owner. The main undesirable result of these unwanted compounds is various types of aggressive algae blooms in the aquarium.

Treating tap water

Treating or pre-treating tap water is not always a great deal of work but some options can be more expensive than others. There are various routes one can take.

You could treat tap water with chlorine in order to kill any bacteria that may be in it. This is a simple option but it is not a very good one for two reasons. Firstly, you will remove most or even all the bacteria but the water will still contain heavy metals like iron and copper and minerals and trace elements such as nitrates and phosphate that will cause algae to flourish. Secondly, you will have to de-chlorinate the water before you can use it because chlorine is also not a friend to your Clownfish and the other marine creatures in your tank or aquarium!

As with so much else, you can choose the way you will obtain the clean, good quality water necessary for your tank:

✓ Use *a basic water filter*. This is the most cost effective option but not necessarily the best one in terms of quality. You can obtain a free-standing filter of some kind or one that fits onto the tap. The latter is less cumbersome and time consuming to use

✓ A *carbon filtration system* is more effective than a regular water filter because these filters remove metals, phenols (acidic, organic compounds) and chlorine. A carbon filter is also said to reduce or even eliminate odours from the water.

There are various types of carbon and carbon-based filters that are commercially available or one could make one.

✓ Perhaps the best type of water filter or filtration system is the *Reverse Osmosis (RO) or Deionization (DI) filtration unit*. The optimal system is thought to be one that is a RO DI combination.

These combined RO/DI systems are expensive but many aquarists believe they are worth the initial cost. The reason is that they save one a great deal by helping to preserve high water quality and so avoid many issues that are both difficult and costly to deal with. In effect, they are thought to pay for themselves.

✓ Instead of filtering water you could *buy fresh, filtered water* from local water companies. It is very important, though, to make sure that the producer and bottler uses a good, reliable filtration system, preferably a RO/DI system of some kind.

✓ In order to avoid both filtering water and adding salt to it you could *buy natural sea water* from a local aquarium, if you are fortunate enough to live near one, or from a company that sells salt water. The third option is to collect water direct from the ocean if you live at the coast.

If you collect seawater yourself, you must choose a location with care so you don't collect water that is contaminated. For example, don't take water from the ocean at a dock or harbour, near a river mouth, close to factories or farmlands or near manufacturing areas. All of these potentially leak or release toxins into the water.

✓ *Buy bottles of distilled water* from commercial companies. The only word of caution here is to ensure that the distiller does not use copper pipes because of they do you may be introducing an undesirable metal into the tank water. You need to make enquiries about distillation processes before you use the water.

One factor to keep in mind when you are deciding on where and how you will get water is the size of the aquarium or tank. Naturally the more water you need the more expensive some options will become. Others will be ruled out simply because they are not feasible or practical for you.

Mixing salt water for your marine or reef tank

Preparing salt water for a tank or aquarium is not complex or difficult. However, getting the salinity levels and therefore the specific gravity right is essential for the health and survival of the marine creatures in the tank. There are a few things that must be kept in mind.

Firstly, one can't use ordinary or common table salt for a salt-water solution for a tank or aquarium. It's also not acceptable to use the various types of sea salt sold in supermarkets. Aquarists have to buy a good quality sea salt mix from a reputable retailer or online shop. There are various websites on the Internet that offer details of the mixes on offer and compare them so that you can choose the best one to meet your needs.

In order to prepare the sea salt mix, you need to use the correct kind of prepared water (as discussed earlier in this chapter). If you are starting out and setting up a new aquarium, you can mix the salt mix into the water in the tank. If you are topping up an existing tank, the solution must be mixed in a bucket or some other clean and suitable container before you add it to the tank water.

When you begin to add the sea salt mix to the water you should begin with less of the mix than you anticipate needing. As with cooking, it is much easier to add more salt than take it out! The mix will also dissolve more quickly if the water is stirred. One should go on mixing until the water clears and no longer looks at all murky or opaque.

In order to assess the salinity or specific gravity levels in the water, you need to use a refractometer or hydrometer. One can't guess or make an estimate; it is essential that the ranges are correct.

If your aquarium or tank only contains fish then the salinity should be between 1.019 and 1.023. However, if you have a reef tank that includes corals the specific gravity range must be between 1.023 and 1.025.

Tips

If you are adding water to a tank that is running, you must also ensure that the water is at the right temperature, not only the correct salinity level. These levels must be as they should be before the water is added to the tank.

Secondly, if you are pouring water into a tank you need to do so very carefully so that the tank inhabitants are not disturbed or stressed and so that the tank's substrate is not disturbed.

Finally, once you have completed the process you should rinse all of the containers and other items you used in fresh water before you put them away so they are ready for use the next time.

3) Topping up the water level in your aquarium

A lower water level in a tank or aquarium is largely due to fresh water evaporation. This would logically indicate that fresh water should be used to top up the tank.

However, it is vital that one check the salinity levels as salt may have also been lost due to other factors such as "salt creep". If the salinity or specific gravity is too low then topping up will need to be with salt water rather than fresh.

4) Dealing with "salt creep"

Salt creep takes place when salt water from a salt or marine tank splashes onto surfaces and items above the water line or even outside the aquarium. Once the water has dried or evaporated, salt crystals are left behind. It is these crystals that cause problems.

The first possible effect of salt creep is that water salinity decreases and unless levels are monitored regularly, this can negatively affect the health and well being of the tank's inhabitants. Fortunately testing specific gravity and adjusting salinity is not too difficult.

These deposits of salt can have serious consequences in and around an aquarium because salt or sodium chloride is a corrosive substance. The nature of the damage depends on the nature of material the salt comes into contact with and how long the exposure lasts for:

- Metal items rust and corrode, releasing toxic compounds

- Electrical items also become corroded and this can cause shorts or burn-outs and loss of power

- Light bulbs that are not in protective housing become encrusted and this reduces the amount of light they give off

- Sheets of plastic, acrylic and glass suffer from an effect called etching. White spots, lines or patches develop in the surface and cause them to become slightly opaque

- Surfaces and items around the aquarium such as carpeting, curtains and wooden surfaces can all be adversely affected as they become mildewed, mouldy or rotted from the damp and corrosive salt. Paintwork may even peel.

The good news is that one can minimise the damage done by salt creep in and around a tank. The golden rule is to remove the salt as quickly as possible; the longer it is in contact with a surface the greater the damage will be. If one deals with salt water splash as part of daily tank maintenance, a great deal of damage caused by salt creep can be avoided.

Steps that help to deal with and counteract the damaging effects of salt creep include:

- ✓ Wipe down the sides of the tank, its stand, light fixtures and the hood or lid with a clean cotton cloth that you have rinsed in fresh water. This should be done regularly.

- ✓ A very small amount of white vinegar on the damp cloth can also be used to reduce etching. However, vinegar can be used on *external tank surfaces only*.

✓ Remove pieces of equipment that can be moved and rinse them off in fresh water.

✓ As part of maintenance, one should wipe down electrical outlet points, plugs and cords using a damp cotton cloth. These should only be wiped down when they have been unplugged.

✓ Keep the water level in the aquarium at or even slightly higher than the tank's trim line. Doing so should reduce etching along the water line.

✓ Place splashboards made of plastic or acrylic or even tiles on the walls close to the aquarium.

✓ Whenever possible, place electrical items at a distance from the aquarium where they are unlikely to get splashed.

✓ Position a plastic mat under the tank to protect carpets and flooring.

Some salt creep is inevitable in some elements of a marine or salt-water tank but at least one can slow it down. By implementing the steps listed above, one can reduce the effects and even prevent unnecessary damage due to salt creep.

5) Standard tank maintenance schedules

Different tank owners will approach tank maintenance differently. The size of the tank and how many fish and invertebrates live in it also affects how often certain tasks must be carried out.

While there may be some differing opinions in terms of when to do what, all aquarists agree that regular, routine maintenance is essential. It can be helpful to break tasks down as follows:

Daily maintenance checklist:

- Check and adjust the water temperature

- Check and adjust salinity

- Remove salt creep

- Ensure all the equipment is running correctly

- Remove uneaten food and other matter that will decay

- Observe all the inhabitants for signs of ill health and stress

- Empty and rinse out the protein skimmer cup

- Check for leaks

- Ensure that all cords and tubes are still correctly connected and not leaking.

Weekly maintenance checklist:

- Test levels of nitrate, ammonia, calcium, phosphate and nitrite and take corrective steps if necessary.

- Test pH levels.

- If you have a lot of marine creatures in your tank you must replace 10% of the water.

- Rinse out pre-filters, filters and the tube running to the protein skimmer.

- Remove any algae from the inside of the tank's sides by scraping it off or by using an algae magnet. These devices can be purchased from reputable retailers.

Bi-weekly to monthly maintenance checklist:

The day before, or two days before, you do any major maintenance work on a tank you must check the pH levels, as they do tend to drop over time. If adjustments are necessary they should be made before you carry out any cleaning, as it will help to guard against pH shock.

Bi-weekly and monthly tasks are:

- Change 10% of the water in the tank or aquarium. A partial water change should in fact be done weekly if you have a lot of marine creatures in the tank.

- Remove algae, deposits and build-up on tank surfaces.

- Remove salt and calcium deposits from the light fixtures. Water in the form of a damp, clean cloth will work to remove salt.

  A small quantity of white vinegar on a clean sponge is effective against calcium.

- Vacuum the substrate to remove any debris.

- Check all equipment such as power sources for salt creep and related damage.

- Check the filters and replace disposable filters that have become dirty, clogged or saturated.

- Clear out the protein skimmer hose and valve. These valves and tubes can also be soaked in vinegar water to remove any calcium. However, they must be very thoroughly rinsed in fresh water afterwards.

Bi-monthly maintenance checklist:

As with bi-weekly and monthly maintenance, one must test and correct pH levels a day or two before working on the aquarium.

- Clean out all tubes, hoses and pipes. Over time, they become clogged by a build-up of compounds and detritus in the tank. An aquarium brush can be used to achieve this. Various sizes and thicknesses of brushes are available commercially.

- Avid and experienced aquarists also clean out important items of equipment such as heaters, Powerheads and pumps.

- Remove any coralline algae growing on submerged tank equipment. This, too, can be achieved by soaking the items in white vinegar, scrubbing them with aquarium brushes and then rinsing them in fresh water.

- If your tank system uses activated charcoal for filtration, the carbon must be replaced. If it is left for too long, the carbon becomes so saturated that it begins to release toxins and impurities back into the water.

Bi-annual and annual maintenance checklist:

- Replace light bulbs or lighting tubes because over time the colour and intensity of the light they provide changes either due to aging in the unit itself or damage from salt creep or calcium build-up.

6) *Being prepared for power failures or outages*

A loss of power is a fact of life for most people. Weather and the state of power grids can impact on the reliability of power supply. Not having power can constitute anything from an inconvenience to a life-threatening situation.

For the creatures in your tank or aquarium, the loss of power is always life threatening. Vital systems for aquarium residents are oxygen and temperature control. Filtration becomes a problem later than these two factors but it too will become crucial. Light is more important for certain invertebrates such as corals than it is for fish. Tank owners must therefore be prepared for a loss of power.

The first option is *battery operated systems*. There is a range of commercially available equipment that runs on batteries. These can provide oxygen, heat and filtration all of which the fish and invertebrates in a tank require in order to survive. These systems are usually the least costly and even the easiest to put in place.

The second possibility is an *Uninterrupted Power Supply* (UPS) unit. These units are traditionally used to keep personal computers going for a while following a loss of power. However, one can also connect essential tank equipment to one. The benefits of a UPS unit are firstly that it'll come on automatically and, secondly, more powerful units can run for longer than battery-operated equipment. The fact that the unit will come on automatically means that your tank's creatures will have emergency help even if you are not at home when the power goes out.

Finally, tank owners could invest in a *power generator*. Given they are not inexpensive to buy, they should be viewed as an investment that will prevent costly livestock losses. As an added advantage, if a larger and more powerful generator is purchased it will have the capacity to meet household power needs in addition to keeping all the aquarium systems running.

Generators are sold in several sizes or capacities and can run on diesel, petrol or even propane. Retailers and suppliers will be able to offer information and advice in terms of the best model and type for your specific requirements.

Regardless of which source of alternative and emergency power you select, it will make a great difference in terms of ensuring your tan's inhabitants stay fit and healthy and reduce your stress levels in the event of a loss of power.

7) A summary of tank conditions

There's a great deal to remember in terms of the parameters for various water and other environmental factors in an aquarium. If various levels and conditions are not correct, a tank owner will be faced with high mortality rates amongst aquarium inhabitants, extra costs and a great deal of extra work.

A summary of the primary levels and parameters for the type of reef tank used for Clownfish are as follows:

- Salinity / Specific Gravity: 1.023 – 1.025

- Temperature: $72 – 78°$ Fahrenheit / $22 – 25°$ Celsius

- pH: 8.1 – 8.4

- Alkalinity: 8 – 12 dKH

- Calcium: 350 – 450 parts per million (ppm)

- Nitrate: Less than 1.0 parts per million (ppm)

- Phosphate: Less than 0.2 parts per million (ppm)

- Magnesium: 1 250 – 1 350 parts per million (ppm)

- Iodine: 0.06 – 0.10 parts per million (ppm)

- Strontium: 8 – 14 parts per million (ppm)

- Ammonia: Should not be detectable

- Nitrite: Should not be detectable

Chapter 10: Feeding your Clownfish

1) What to feed your Clownfish

In the wild, the Clownfish is an opportunistic feeder and not a predator. In other words, it will eat whatever food it comes across rather than hunting for it. These fish are also omnivorous and therefore eat both plant and animal matter.

As such, the Clownfish's diet consists of a range of items, most of which are provided by its host anemone or by chance: food particles left by the anemone after it has eaten, parasites on the host's body, dead anemone tentacles, small crustaceans and molluscs, some algae, plankton and even undigested excrement.

The fact that they are omnivores and opportunistic and therefore enjoy a range of types of foods makes these fish much easier to feed than many other species. You can feed Clownfish frozen, live, flake or even tablet-form foods.

Experienced aquarists recommend a good quality marine flake food that is combined with a mixture of frozen and live foods. These can include krill, bloodworms, finely chopped meat, shrimp or Mysis and spirulina flakes (which are made from highly nutritious blue-green algae).

It's important that their diet also includes vegetable matter. These fish graze on algae in between feeds so one should see to it that there is some available in the aquarium.

2) How often to feed Clownfish

Here again, there is debate and differing opinions with some tank owners only feeding Clownfish every second day (although this may slow their growth), some claiming that once a day is the minimum and yet other aquarists feeding their fish 3 or even 4 times a day. There is consensus, however, that certain factors play a role.

Factors that will affect this are:

- The size of Clownfish species you have

- How much food you dispense at a time

- How many marine creatures there are in the tank

- The feeding routine that works best for you and your fish and invertebrates.

A point on which all aquarium owners do however agree is that frozen foods must be thawed or defrosted before they are given to fish.

3) How much food to give your Clownfish

There are guidelines one can use in order to determine how much food to give your Clownfish. If you feed them once a day, give them what they will eat in about 5 minutes. If you give them food two or three times during the day, it should not be more than they can eat in approximately 3 minutes.

4) Dealing with excess food or leftovers

Uneaten food that remains in the tank and floats around in the water and/or gets stuck in cracks and crevices pose a health risk in the tank. This type of debris is dangerous because it can lead to algae blooms, bacterial outbreaks and reduction in overall water quality.

A detritus pack or clean-up crew in the form of starfish, crabs such as hermit crabs and various types of marine snails help a great deal with this issue.

Chapter 11: Health management

Setting up a reef or salt-water tank for your Clownfish is time consuming and costly business. Once it has been done and you are carrying out routine maintenance, the last thing you want is an outbreak of disease in your aquarium.

Apart from selecting stock with care and monitoring your marine creature's health, there is another step you can take: make use of a quarantine tank.

1) A quarantine tank

What is a quarantine tank for?

Most aquarists or tank owners don't have a quarantine tank because of the expense of setting one up and the maintenance. However, quarantine tanks don't need to be big or costly. Furthermore the benefits these tanks provide mean that they in effect pay for themselves.

Quarantine tanks, as the name implies, keep new or sick fish or other marine creatures away from the others in order to prevent the spread of infections, parasites or other medical problems.

However, these tanks have a second, very important function and that is that they make it easier to treat or medicate sick fish. This second function of these tanks gives rise to their alternative names of treatment or hospital tanks.

When you are dealing with an infected fish, you need to do two things. Firstly, the infected fish or fishes must be kept away from the healthy ones. Secondly, you need to be able to medicate the sick fish without exposing well fish to medications that could harm them. Some fish medications can be particularly harmful to some invertebrates.

By using a quarantine tank, you can achieve both of these objectives and deal with the medical problem faster and without knock-on effects in the tank and on the tank's general population.

When a quarantine tank should be used

These important tanks are used on two different occasions. The fist time a quarantine tank is important or useful is when you buy new stock for your tank. A quarantine tank allows you to isolate fish and invertebrates before you introduce them into the main aquarium. This gives you the opportunity to make sure that the newcomers are healthy. The second situation is when you discover a new fish or invertebrate or one in the main tank is sick.

Further benefits of quarantine tanks

There is a range of additional benefits associated with these tanks. Firstly, because quarantine tanks are usually fairly small (often about 10 gallons or 45.5 UK litres or 38 US litres or slightly more), one uses less medication and can monitor and control dosing far more easily. This also greatly reduces the risk of accidental overdosing. All these factors make treatment more effective and save you some money.

In addition, it is much easier to watch and examine a sick fish or other marine creature in a smaller and less populated tank. One can assess physical factors such as colour, eyes, the condition of fins and scales, growths and so forth.

With both sick and newly arrived marine creatures, a quarantine tank offers an ideal opportunity to make sure they are eating well and even what foods they respond to better. Again, this is much harder or even impossible to do in a large or main tank.

Finally, a quarantine tank acts as a halfway house for new-comers where they can start to settle and recover from the stress of transport or shipping before moving into the main tank. This often makes acclimation to the main tank easier.

Setting up a quarantine tank

The equipment required for a quarantine tank is essentially a much reduced or streamlined version of what is needed for the large or main tank. In addition to the tank itself, one needs to buy substrate, a filter, a thermometer, an air pump, a heater and suitable lighting.

One must also have a dedicated water test kit and aquarium nets for use in the quarantine tank as one can't use any equipment from it in the main tank or vice versa as this creates the risk of contaminating the main tank and its inhabitants.

It's a good idea to have a quarantine tank that is bare because porous materials such as rocks, sand and gravel can absorb medications. This means that your fish are not receiving the correct dose. Because some fish like Clownfish like or need to have hiding places you will need to supply some. However, they should be made of non-porous materials or items such as sections of plastic pipe, for example.

Why quarantine corals?

As with fish, there are two primary reasons to place new corals in a quarantine tank.

As they do for fish, these tanks offer corals a place to recover from the stress of being transported, settle and get used to their new environment. In this way-station tankm the corals have an opportunity to acclimate to the new water and lighting.

Corals are prone to a host of parasites that you don't want in your main tank. If you place new corals in a dedicated quarantine tank when you first get them you will be able to examine them for presence of Limpets, undesirable Red Bugs and snail species, Flatworms and Nudibranchs.

One knows that corals are free of pests and parasites if, after a period in quarantine, they open or expand as they should and are colourful.

Quarantine tank maintenance

Ideally, one should have one quarantine tank for fish and another for corals. It's also extremely important that the quarantine tank and equipment is disinfected between uses. A mild (2-5%) chlorine bleach solution is an effective disinfectant for this purpose. However, one must ensure that all the chlorine is removed before using the tank again.

The quarantine tank and all the associated equipment must also be thoroughly dried because drying kills many aquatic pathogens but certainly not all of them.

2) Common Clownfish illnesses and health problems

Common signs of illness in Clown and other fish

While one can acquire the knowledge to make a much more accurate diagnosis in terms of the health issue a fish is suffering from, there are some general signs and symptoms all tank owners should be on the look-out for:

- Loss of, or marked reduction in, appetite
- Growths or lumps
- Listlessness
- Unusual or erratic movements
- White spots or fungus on the body
- White patches in the mouth
- Laboured or unusual breathing.

If you run the usual water quality and parameter tests and they are all as they should be, then you need to establish what specifically the fish is suffering from. If you don't feel up to the task, a vet or marine specialist should be consulted.

Preventing common health problems

There are steps that one can and should take that go a very long way to guarding against the common health issues that fish, including Clownfish, are susceptible to:

- ✓ Use a quarantine tank to screen new fish and isolate and treat sick fish

- ✓ Maintain good water quality through testing, dosing when needed, regular partial water changes, maintaining the correct pH and salinity levels

- ✓ Ensure effective filtration, correct water temperature and lighting levels and adequate oxygenation

- ✓ Don't put too many fish in a tank as overcrowding causes stress-related problems and cross infection

- ✓ Perform all the necessary maintenance on the tank to ensure optimal conditions at all times

- ✓ Use appropriate foods and feeding routines.

Fish diseases and ailments

A) Cryptocaryon irritans

Cryptocaryon is more commonly known as White Spot Disease or Marine Ichthyophthirius (Ich). It is caused by a protozoan (a single celled organism) called *Cryptocaryon irritans*, which infests fish by burrowing into their skin and later the gills and forms cysts.

It is not a rapidly progressing illness and if it is detected early it can be very successfully treated. However, if it is neglected, the consequences are very serious and can destroy an entire fish population and infest the entire tank.

The life cycle of Cryptocaryon irritans

The life cycle of this protozoan is significant both in terms of the effect on the infected fish and why it poses such a huge risk to all the fish in a tank.

The earliest stage of the life of *Cryptocaryon irritans* is when the immature cells, called tomites, are released when the cyst in the host bursts. These tomites float in the water until they find a new host and attach themselves to it.

The next stage in the life cycle is that of a parasitic trophont. These nasty organisms burrow into the flesh or gills of the host fish and begin to feed on the tissue at that site.

Once the trophont has consumed enough, it forms a cyst. These are called inactive tomonts. The cysts may be stuck in the surface mucous of the fish or buried deep in their tissue.

Within 6 to 10 days the cells inside the cysts reproduce. Each one becomes a tomite. When the cyst is mature it ruptures and releases hundreds of tomites into the water. Each one will search for a host.

In other words, the cycle repeats itself and the only difference is that each time there are more tomites. It is easy to see how easily an entire tank can become infected.

Symptoms

The first sign of White Spot Disease or Marine Ich are very small white spots on the fins and body of the fish that is host to *Cryptocaryon irritans*. These spots can be as small as grains of salt, which is why a tank owner must be vigilant and observe and monitor fish regularly. This protozoan only moves from the skin to the gills when it has reached the parasitic trophont stage.

Infected fish will also rub themselves against objects in the tank. This is an effort to dislodge the parasites on their skin. When the parasites have attacked the fish's gills the symptoms become far more marked and severe. The gills become blocked by mucous, tissue debris and the tomonts themselves. This results in laboured breathing.

At this advanced stage, the fish will have stopped eating, will be very listless and have lost colour in the places where the trophonts destroyed pigment cells in the skin.

There will also be lesions or wounds in the skin, which then become infected by other bacteria.

Treatment of Marine Ich

Treatment needs to be effective for each stage of the life cycle of the *Cryptocaryon irritans*. Not all treatment options work on more than one stage. For example, copper effectively combats the free-swimming tomites but does nothing to deal with trophonts that have burrowed into tissue. To deal with this advanced stage of the infestation one needs to use a combination of formalin and freshwater treatments. These are administered over an extended period through baths and dips.

A quarantine tank is essential to deal with this problem. You need to generate vigorous aeration in the tank as part of the treatment. Two containers of different types of treatment water also need to be prepared.

In the first one, the water should include a formalin product. It is vital that one follows the directions on the packaging so that the solution is correctly mixed. This is the treatment water. It should also contain another product in addition to the formalin that will counteract the ammonia that is a harmful and inevitable by-product of this treatment process. High levels will cause a condition known as ammonia burn.

If you don't have a formalin treatment product, emergency treatment can be provided in the form of a freshwater bath. It won't cure the infestation but it can give a sick fish some relief by flushing some mucous out of the gills and removing some parasites from the skin. This eases breathing and reduces irritation. Place the fish in the hyposalinity dip and then back in the quarantine tank. A suitable formalin solution should be obtained as soon as possible.

The second container should contain water with lowered salinity. Hyposalinity or the lowering of specific gravity to approximately 1.010 ppm won't treat or cure the infestation but it does help to prevent re-infestation. It is also used as a dip for fish that have been in the treatment water. This low salinity water helps to remove dead or weak parasites or mucous from the affected fish.

The treatment process must be handled carefully and accurately as fish requiring these steps are already very sick – perhaps even dying – and weak.

The first stage is to gently place the infested fish into the container containing the formalin treatment product. The sicker the fish, the more careful one must be. A seriously infested fish may not be able to tolerate the treatment bath for more than a few minutes if at all or may even die during the treatment.

When dealing with such badly affected fish, another option is to dilute the solution further, which may make a longer dip time possible. Less badly affected fish can remain in the treatment bath longer (anything up to an hour).

The stage after the treatment bath is a dip in the second container that contains low salinity water. A very stressed or shocked fish may only cope with a 30 second dip. Less severely affected fish can tolerate 1 minute or even 2 minutes. Once this dip is finished, the fish should be returned to the quarantine tank.

Fish affected by *Cryptocaryon irritans* should be kept in the quarantine tank for the duration of the life cycle of the protozoan/a minimum of 4 weeks. The treatment will continue as directed by the formalin product manufacturers. It is also recommended that an antibacterial be added to the treatment regimen so that one also deals with secondary bacterial infections.

During the period that you are treating your fish, there should be no fish in the main tank. This will ensure that all the protozoa, at each cycle of their life, in the tank die off as they are unable to find fish hosts.

Words of caution:

- Don't leave fish unattended in the treatment bath or the dip. You need to watch them closely and constantly and remove them immediately if they show signs of distress or stress.

- Formaldehyde is a toxic substance and should be used with caution and due care. It should only be used as directed, for parasite infestations and fungal diseases in fish. It is highly toxic to invertebrates and can be harmful to fish if they are exposed to it too often.

- Ensure that the treatment product you select is effective against *Cryptocaryon* specifically as some are for other types of Ich but are not effective against this protozoan.

Preventing re-infestation

If you don't eliminate the *Cryptocaryon irritans* from the main tank, your fish will be re-infested regardless of how effectively you treated the fish themselves. As previously mentioned, the main tank must not house any fish for at least 4 weeks.

Creating hyposalinity in the tank speeds up the *Cryptocaryon's* life cycle which helps while you dose the tank water. However, one can only use this technique if your tank is fish only tank or not a reef tank. Hyposalinity is not an option if you have corals and various types of invertebrates. There are various solutions available for reef tanks that can be added to the water to destroy *Cryptocaryon* at each stage of the life cycle.

Before you can reintroduce your fish back into the main tank, you must change filtering materials, clean filters very thoroughly and do a full water change. Then run a full battery of tests to ensure that all the water and environmental parameters are correct.

B) Brooklynella

Brooklynella is more commonly known as Clownfish Disease. Despite this common name, it is not only Clownfish that become infested. This disease is another form of Ich and is caused by a protozoan (a single celled organism) called *Brooklynella hostilis,* which infests fish by burrowing into their skin and later the gills and forming cysts.

Brooklynella, unlike *Cryptocaryon,* is a very rapidly progressing illness and can kill a fish within a few hours or days. This means that immediate diagnosis and treatment is essential to prevent the loss of all the fish in the tank.

Symptoms

The signs and symptoms of this aggressive disease are dramatic and distressing to see. *Brooklynella,* again unlike *Cryptocaryon,* attacks the gills first. In its efforts to dislodge the parasite, a fish will scrape against rocks, corals or other hard surfaces.

As the gills become increasingly affected, fish begin to breathe rapidly and will gasp for air at the surface of the water. It will usually remain near the surface or where there is a strong stream of water entering the tank. This inability to breathe is due to a build-up of thick mucous that clogs the gills. Hardly surprisingly fish with *Brooklynella* stop eating, their colour fades and they become very lethargic.

The most distinctive symptom of this very serious fish disease begins as the disease progresses: the heavy production of slime or mucous that covers the fish's body. This thick, white coating begins at the head and then spreads to the rest of the body. This is often accompanied by lesions on the skin. These lesions often become infected by bacteria and need separate treatment.

Treatment

Treatment recommendations include a solution of malachite green or copper sulphate used in conjunction with formaldehyde. However, many aquarists believe the most effective treatment for *Brooklynella* is formaldehyde used on its own along with a hyposalinity dip. Treatment should be administered over an extended period.

A quarantine tank is essential to deal with this problem. You need to generate vigorous aeration in the tank as part of the treatment. Two containers of different types of treatment water also need to be prepared.

In the first one, the water should include a formalin product. It is vital that one follows the directions on the packaging so that the solution is correctly mixed. This is the treatment water. It should also contain another product in addition to the formalin that will counteract the ammonia that is a harmful and inevitable by-product of this treatment process. High levels will cause a condition known as ammonia burn.

If you don't have a formalin treatment product, emergency treatment can be provided in the form of a freshwater bath. It won't cure the infestation but it can give a sick fish some relief by flushing some mucous out of the gills and removing some parasites from the skin. This eases breathing and reduces irritation. Place the fish in the hyposalinity dip and then back in the quarantine tank. A suitable formalin solution should be obtained as soon as possible.

The second container should contain water with lowered salinity. Hyposalinity or the lowering of specific gravity to approximately 1.010 ppm won't treat or cure the infestation but it does help to prevent re-infestation. It is also used as a dip for fish that have been in the treatment water. This low salinity water helps to remove dead or weak parasites and some mucous from the affected fish.

The treatment process must be handled carefully and accurately as fish requiring these steps are already very sick – perhaps even dying – and weak.

The first stage is to gently place the infested fish or fishes into the container containing the formalin treatment product. The sicker the fish, the more careful one must be. A seriously infested fish may not be able to tolerate the treatment bath for more than a few minutes if at all or may even die during the treatment.

When dealing with such sick and weak fish, another option is to dilute the solution further, which may make a longer dip time possible. Less badly affected fish can remain in the treatment bath longer (anything up to an hour).

The stage after the treatment bath is a dip in the second container that contains low salinity water. A very stressed or shocked fish may only cope with a 30 second dip. Less severely affected fish can tolerate 1 minute or even 2 minutes. Once this dip is finished, the fish should be returned to the quarantine tank.

Fish affected by *Brooklynella* should be kept in the quarantine tank for the duration of the life cycle of the protozoan or at least 4 weeks. The treatment will continue as directed by the formalin product manufacturers. It is also strongly recommended that an antibacterial be added to the treatment regimen so that one also deals with secondary bacterial infections.

During the period that you are treating your fish, there should be no fish in the main tank. This will ensure that all the protozoa, at each cycle of their life, in the tank die off as they are unable to find fish hosts.

Words of caution:

- Don't leave fish unattended in the treatment bath or the dip. You need to watch them closely and constantly and remove them immediately if they show signs of distress or stress.

- Formaldehyde is a toxic substance and should be used with caution and due care. It should only be used as directed, for parasite infestations and fungal diseases in fish. It is highly toxic to invertebrates and can be harmful to fish if they are exposed to it too often.

- Ensure that the treatment product you select is effective against *Brooklynella* specifically as some are for other types of Ich but are not effective against this protozoan.

C) Oodinium

Oodinium, also known as Velvet Disease or Coral Fish Disease, is caused by a dinoflagellate (a protist or parasitic, single-celled microorganism) called *Amyloodinium ocellatum*. This nasty type of infestation is another of the Ich diseases.

Amyloodinium, like *Brooklynella*, is a very rapidly progressing illness and can kill a fish within a few hours or days. This organism also reproduces very quickly. This means that immediate diagnosis and treatment is essential to prevent the loss of all the fish in the tank.

Symptoms

The symptoms of *Amyloodinium* are very similar to those of *Brooklynella* infestation and this organism also attacks the fish's gills first.

An infected fish will scrape against rocks, corals or other hard surfaces in an effort to dislodge the parasites. As the gills become increasingly affected, fish begin to breathe rapidly and will gasp for air at the surface of the water. One often notices breathing difficulties when fish stay at the surface or where there is a flow of water. This inability to breathe is due to a build-up of mucous that clogs the gills. The fish will stop eating, their colour fades and they become very lethargic.

Unlike with *Cryptocaryon*, *Amyloodinium* starts in the gills and then spreads to the body. Tiny cysts on the fish's body and fins become visible. They look like grains of salt and resemble the first sign of White Spot Disease/Marine Ich or *Cryptocaryon*.

What is different, however, is that these cysts at this advanced stage of the disease give the fish a tan or golden colouring and a velvet-like film coats the whole fish, which is what gives rise to the name Velvet Disease. The fish's eyes will also cloud over in the final stage of the disease.

The life cycle of Amyloodinium or Oodinium

Like *Cryptocaryon, Amyloodinium ocellatum* has 3 stages in its life cycle.

The first stage in the life cycle is when free-swimming cells, called dinospores, are released when a mature cyst in the host bursts. These dinospores float in the water until they find a new host and they can survive for up to 8 days without a host. Some strains can survive for a month in cooler water.

In the next stage of the life cycle, the dinospores loose their ability to swim. They become parasitic trophozoites, which attach to their host by means of a feeding filament. They attack the gill tissue of the fish and begin to feed on it. The trophozoite will feed off its host for 3 to 7 days at which point they are mature. They may drop off the host, remain in the mucous membrane covering the host or stay buried in the host's flesh. The trophozoites remaining in the fish then form cysts.

At the encysted stage, the organism is called a tomont. Within 5 days, the cells inside the cysts reproduce. When the cyst is mature it, ruptures and releases hundreds of tomites or dinospores into the water. Each one will search for a host.

The life cycle then repeats and the only difference is that each time there are more free-swimming dinospores. An entire tank can become infected very quickly.

Treatment

Treatment needs to be effective for each stage of the life cycle of the *Amyloodinium*. Not all treatment options work on more than one stage. To deal with the advanced stage of the infestation one needs to use a combination of treatments. These are administered over an extended period through baths and dips.

A quarantine tank is essential to deal with this problem. Two containers of different types of treatment water also need to be prepared. *Amyloodinium* can survive a broad salinity range (anything from 3 to 45 ppm). As a result, a hyposalinity dip or bath is not at all effective against this parasite.

In the first container, the water should include a formalin or formalin and copper solution product. It is vital that one follows the directions on the packaging so that the solution is correctly mixed. This is the treatment water. It should also contain another product in addition to the formalin that will counteract the ammonia that is a harmful and inevitable by-product of this treatment process. High levels will cause a condition known as ammonia burn.

If you don't have a treatment product, emergency treatment can be provided in the form of a freshwater bath. It won't cure the infestation but it can give a sick fish some relief. A suitable treatment solution should be obtained as soon as possible.

The second container should contain a freshwater dip. This water should have a slightly reduced pH and a specific gravity of 1.001. Some aquarists also add the compound known as Methylene Blue.

The first stage is to place the infected fish into the treatment water. A severely infested fish may not be able to tolerate the treatment bath for more than a few minutes if at all or may even die during the treatment.

When dealing with such badly affected fish another option is to dilute the solution further, which may make a longer dip time possible. Less badly affected fish can remain in the treatment bath longer (anything up to an hour).

The stage after the treatment bath is a dip in the second container that holds the fresh water solution as described above. An effective duration for the dip is between 3 and 5 minutes. Don't worry if a fish appears dead and even 'lies down'. This behaviour is a normal initial reaction to being in the fresh water solution. After a minute or two the fish should perk up significantly.

There are two reasons why a freshwater solution is so effective against this parasite. The first is that with *Amyloodinium* the cysts are not as deeply embedded as they are in cases of *Cryptocaryon*. Secondly, the membrane of the cells of the Oodinium cyst isn't strong enough to withstand the change in osmotic pressure caused by a move to fresh water.

As a result of this pressure, the cysts burst. However, in order to achieve this, the fish must remain in the dip for 3 minutes. Once this dip is finished the fish should be returned to the quarantine tank.

Fish affected by *Amyloodinium* should be kept in the quarantine tank for the duration of the life cycle of the parasite. The treatment will continue as directed by the treatment product manufacturers. It is also recommended that an antibacterial be added to the treatment regimen so that one also deals with secondary bacterial infections.

During the period that you are treating your fish, there should be no fish in the main tank. This will ensure that all the dinospores and cysts in the tank die.

Preventing re-infection

If you don't eliminate *Amyloodinium* from the main tank, your fish will be re-infested regardless of how effectively you treated the fish themselves. As previously mentioned, the main tank must not house any fish for at least 4 weeks.

Raising the tank temperature to 85 or even 90° Fahrenheit or 29.5 to 32° Celsius will speed up the life cycle. There are also various solutions available for reef tanks that can be added to the water to destroy *Amyloodinium* dinospores.

Before you can reintroduce your fish back into the main tank, you must change filtering materials, clean filters very thoroughly and do a full water change. Then run a full battery of tests to ensure that all the water and environmental parameters are correct.

Words of caution:

- Don't leave fish unattended in the treatment bath or the dip. You need to watch them closely and constantly and remove them immediately if they show signs of distress or stress.

- Formaldehyde is a toxic substance and should be used with caution and due care. It should only be used as directed, for parasite infestations and fungal diseases in fish. It is highly toxic to invertebrates and can be harmful to fish if they are exposed to it too often.

- Ensure that the treatment product you select is effective against *Amyloodinium* specifically as some are for other types of Ich but are not effective against this parasite.

D) Tail Rot and Fin Rot

Tail and Fin Rot is thought to be caused by injuries such as nipping by other fish, poor tank conditions or a bacterial infection following injury. They can also be a secondary condition caused by Fish Tuberculosis.

Symptoms

The signs and symptoms of Fin or Tail Rot are easy to spot. The tail and/or fin look frayed and show signs of disintegration. In very severe cases the tail and fins can be reduced to stumps because the tissue has broken down entirely.

Other signs are bleeding along the edges of the fins or tail, red or inflamed-looking areas at the base of the tail or fin, exposed fin rays (the soft, flexible 'rods' that run the length of the fin) and ulcers on the skin. In fish with advanced Rot their eyes also become cloudy.

Treatment

Given there are several possible causes of Tail and Fin Rot, the first steps must be to establish the cause and place the affected fish in a quarantine tank. Once the cause has been determined, one must remedy it if possible and treat the fish or the water. For example, if the damage is due to attacks by another fish, you will have to take steps to keep them apart, or if water quality is poor that must be remedied immediately.

Regardless of the cause, you will probably have to use an antibiotic treatment; even if the rot is not bacterial in origin, the damaged tissue will almost certainly be infected. The choice one has at this point is to either dose the fish or the water.

If an antibiotic is added to the water is it very important that the instructions are carefully followed with regards to dosage. In addition, be very cautious about adding medications to a main tank as they may adversely affect invertebrates and corals.

If the antibiotic is to be administered to the fish, one can mix it carefully in to flake food. Some aquarists suggest that one keeps fish a little hungry so that when the flakes mixed with antibiotic arrive, they are eaten fast and the antibiotic is not lost into the water.

Your local marine specialist or vet will be able to offer advice as to which antibiotic would be most suitable and to suggest an appropriate dose. Chloromycetin and Tetracyclines are quite often used in very small quantities.

E) Black Spot Disease

Black Spot Disease is caused by small parasitic worms. It gets its name from the black spots formed by the parasites. These marks are not nearly as numerous as the white ones characteristic of White Spot Disease or Marine Ich. It is also not nearly as serious, although parasites are never desirable!

Symptoms

Other than the black spots on the fish's body, which are the primary sign, the other symptom is that the fish will move erratically and try to remove the irritating parasites by rubbing against hard surfaces such as rocks.

Treatment

If a fish is not badly infested, a 5 minute bath in freshwater should be enough to deal with these parasites. As with any treatment, the fish should be watched closely and removed as soon as it shows signs of becoming highly stressed.

For fish suffering from a more severe infestation, treatment with a solution of trichlorofon or copper is necessary. A copper- or trichlorofon-based solution can't be added to the main tank, as it will adversely affect invertebrates. The fish that require treatment must therefore be placed in a quarantine tank first.

Prevention

Placing new fish in a freshwater dip and then keeping them in a quarantine tank for a few weeks before introducing them to the main tank is one of the primary ways to ensure that this parasite is not introduced into your tank.

In addition, ensuring that the water quality is good at all times and that the other environmental parameters in the tank are always as they should be will prevent stress in the tank inhabitants. Stress affects fish badly, as it damages their mucous coating. Weaknesses in this coating make the fish vulnerable as parasites can gain hold far more easily.

Finally, the use of a correctly installed ultraviolet (UV) sterilizer will also help to prevent outbreaks of this parasite.

F) Gill and Fin Flukes

These flukes are small, worm-like parasites that multiply very quickly. This is a highly infectious disease that is fatal if affected fish are not treated very quickly. What makes this parasite so dangerous is that they can clog the gills of the fish, which causes them to suffocate slowly.

Symptoms

As with other parasitic infestations, the affected fish will swim erratically and rub against hard surfaces as they try to dislodge the parasites. Fish with these flukes also exhibit rapid and laboured breathing and often have white patches on their bodies and cloudy eyes.

In severe cases, the worm-like parasites may sometimes be visible as thin, thread-like objects.

Treatment

A freshwater bath usually kills the majority of the parasites and brings the fish immediate relief from many of the symptoms. For fish that are more severely affected a longer treatment bath of salt water and methylene blue may be required.

Prevention

Placing new fish in a freshwater dip and then keeping them in a quarantine tank for a few weeks before introducing them to the main tank is one of the primary ways to ensure that this parasite is not introduced into your tank.

In addition, ensuring that the water quality is good at all times and that the other environmental parameters in the tank are always as they should be will prevent stress in the tank inhabitants. Stress affects fish badly as it damages their mucous coating. Weaknesses in this coating make the fish vulnerable as parasites can gain hold far more easily.

Finally, the use of a correctly installed ultraviolet (UV) sterilizer will also help to prevent outbreaks of this parasite.

G) Lymphocystis

Lymphocystis is a fish disease that is caused by a virus. It is also known as Cauliflower Disease because of the appearance of the growths. While fish that have this problem look really ill, the condition is rarely fatal. In addition, it may even clear up on its own if the water quality is high.

Symptoms

The only symptom is the clumps of wart-like growths (that look like cauliflowers) that grow on the body of fish with this virus.

Treatment

Like with most viruses, there is no treatment for Lymphocystis. One can give fish a short freshwater dip but essentially the condition will go with time *if* water quality is optimal. The danger with viral conditions is the possibility of secondary bacterial infections. If this occurs, the fish should be placed in a quarantine tank and dosed with antibiotics.

Prevention

Placing new fish in a freshwater dip and then keeping them in a quarantine tank for a few weeks before introducing them to the main tank is one of the primary ways to ensure that this virus is not introduced into your tank.

Ensuring that high water quality is maintained in the tank at all times is the best deterrent for this condition.

In addition, ensuring that the water quality is good at all times and that the other environmental parameters in the tank are always as they should be will prevent stress in the tank inhabitants. Stress affects fish badly and makes them more likely to contract a viral infection.

H) Marine Fungus

This disease, also called Ichthyophonus or CNS Disease, is usually associated with stress. It is also sometimes caused by poor water quality. This is fortunately not a very common disease, yet treatment is very difficult. The fungus is usually introduced into the tank when new marine creatures are introduced into it.

Symptoms

Fish suffering from this fungus develop skin that looks like sandpaper. They also darken in colour, become listless and have poor appetites.

Treatment

Treating this condition is not easy. Affected fish must be placed in a quarantine tank and dosed with a suitable anti-fungal medication. Your local retailer or vet will be able to recommend suitable products. One must also ensure that water quality is good and that the fish is as stress-free as possible.

Prevention

Ensuring that high water quality is maintained and that all the environmental factors are optimal at all times is the best deterrent for this condition.

Correct water quality and environmental parameters will prevent stress in the tank inhabitants. Stress affects fish badly, as it breaks down the mucous coating the fish's skin and thereby makes them more vulnerable and likely to develop fungal problems.

Placing new fish in a freshwater dip and then keeping them in a quarantine tank for a few weeks before introducing them to the main tank is one of the primary ways to ensure that this virus is not introduced into your tank.

I) *Mycobacterium marinum or Fish Tuberculosis*

Mycobacterium marinum is also known as Fish Tuberculosis (TB). It is a very serious and invariably fatal bacterial infection. Not only does it pose a huge risk to fish, but also fish tank owners or aquarists can contract it too and suffer some serious health problems as a result.

These aggressive bacteria can survive in salt and fresh water, in soil and without a host for extended periods of time.

Symptoms

Fish that have contracted *Mycobacterium marinum* are affected in several dramatic ways. They loose colour and scales. They suffer from wasting and therefore become very thin. In addition, they develop lesions on the skin and may develop skeletal deformities the most obvious one being curvature of the spine.

Treatment

This serious illness is almost impossible to cure. Many aquarists believe it is kinder to euthanize a fish rather than let it suffer the ravages of the disease and the stress of treatments that are unlikely to help. The best way to prevent it spreading is drastic: euthanizing all the fish in the tank!

Apart from a desire to spare the fish suffering, aquarists are also reluctant to treat these fish as it exposes them to the bacteria and possible infection.

The medication that is usually used to treat this infection is Kanamycin/Kantrex. As with other forms of TB, treatment involves a combination of medications (at least 2), which are administered over an extended period, which is usually a minimum of three months. Delightful

The usual 'fixes' such as raising the water temperature, changing the water or raising salinity levels don't have any effect at all on *Mycobacterium marinum*, which thrives in warm water.

Prevention

The difficulty with treatment and the resulting high mortality rates make prevention very important with this disease. The first step in prevention is to keep fish happy/stress-free and well fed, as this will promote strong immunity. They will be more likely to be able to resist infection, at least initially.

Weak or injured fish are extremely vulnerable and should be moved into treatment or quarantine tanks as soon as possible if they show signs of the illness.

New fish must be placed in quarantine for several weeks before they are introduced into the main tank. All of the décor and the equipment that goes into the tanks must be sterilised.

If an entire aquarium and fish population has been affected by this highly infectious disease, it is essential that the tank be emptied and cleaned very thoroughly with bleach, rinsed with great care and then left to dry. It should not be restocked until the tank has been cleaned and is dry.

J) Popeye

Popeye is a condition rather than a disease. It is also known as Exopthalmia or Exophthalmos and can be caused by eye trauma or by fungal or bacterial infection/disease.

Trauma can be the result of a scrape, bump or a scratch. Fish can injure themselves on objects in the tank, get hurt during fights with other fish, and tank owners can accidentally damage fish's eyes when using an aquarium net. In the case of trauma, it is usually only one eye that is affected. An eye injury can look alarming but often doesn't impact on the overall health of the fish.

In the case of infections of some kind, the fish can be far more badly affected in terms of its general health and its ability and desire to feed. Both eyes may also be affected.

The third possible cause of eye problems, including eye infections, is a range of environmental factors:

- Poor water quality
- Contaminated items are introduced into the tank
- The water temperature is too high
- The levels of harmful compounds such as nitrates are above acceptable parameters
- The fish are stressed
- The fish are receiving poor or inadequate nutrition.

Symptoms

Popeye makes the eye look as though it is under pressure and bulging or about to pop out of the socket. Some conditions also make the eye look clouded or opaque.

Treatment for trauma-induced Popeye

The affected fish poses no risk to the other fish in the main tank, as it is not infectious. Handling the fish will probably only worsen the injury. However, if the trauma is due to bullying by another fish, it would be wise to separate them. In addition, if the injury is severe the fish must be placed in the quarantine tank for treatment.

Minor injuries will heal on their own over time, but treatment is required for more serious injuries. Aquarists recommend the use of a broad-spectrum antibiotic that is mixed into flake food. This will combat any infection that may start in the wound. Using a liquid vitamin is also suggested and your vet or retailer will be able to advise you on the most appropriate products to use. Eventually the eye will return to normal size.

However, with more serious injuries or where treatment has not been effective the fish may suffer very significant permanent effects. The fish may loose the sight in the affected eye. In this situation the eye will look grey, opaque or even completely colourless.

With very severe eye injuries that go untreated, or where the treatment was not effective, the eye may disappear or burst. The shock and trauma of this can be fatal to the fish.

If both eyes are affected and the fish looses or partially looses its vision, it will be unable to feed properly and will not survive. Many tank owners prefer to use euthanasia rather than leave a blind fish to slowly and painfully starve to death.

Treatment for infection or disease-induced Popeye

Popeye can also be a symptom, or one of the symptoms, of an underlying medical condition, such as an internal fungal or bacterial infection such as Vibriosis or kidney disease. In these situations, both eyes are likely to be affected.

If the Popeye is treated, rather than the underlying illness *and* the Popeye, then the eye condition naturally won't improve and the fish may die of the underlying medical issue or complications caused by it.

A fish with infection or disease-related Popeye must be removed from the general population and placed in a quarantine tank for treatment. Once in 'hospital', both medical issues can be dealt with.

If eye problems can be attributed to poor water quality, 5 to 10% of the tank water must be changed daily. The water must be tested regularly and steps taken to correct any problems. This routine must be continued until the eye conditions have cleared.

K) Vibriosis

Vibriosis is a bacterial disease that attacks the gastrointestinal tract / the digestive system. The bacterium that causes this illness is *Vibrio anguillarum* (*Vibrio anguillarium*). This is a serious and aggressive disease that progresses rapidly. Infection is the result of ingesting the bacteria in food.

Symptoms

Fish suffering from Vibriosis display a wide range of signs and symptoms. However, not all fish survive long enough to develop all of them.

Some signs are loss of appetite, lethargy, red or bloody streaks under the skin that become dark and swollen lesions that ooze pus, red spots on the body and cloudy eyes that may turn into Popeye. The tell-tale streaks and subsequent ulcers are the only symptom some fish display.

Treatment

Treatment must be given rapidly in an effort to save the fish that are infected and prevent further infections.

Fish with Vibriosis must be placed in a quarantine tank to avoid infecting their tank-mates. The sick fish and the water in the tank must be dosed with an antibiotic that will kill gram-negative bacteria (Erythromycin, for example). One must also use a broad-spectrum bactericide and Potassium Permanganate as they will reduce the levels of free-floating bacteria in the water.

Increased salinity or specific gravity has no effect on this bacterium because it survives easily in saltwater. One must also do a 50% water change in the main tank as soon as possible. Find out from your vet what bactericide you can use in the main tank that won't affect corals and invertebrates adversely.

Preventing re-infection

Performing all the necessary routine maintenance on your tank will go a long way to helping avoid bacterial outbreaks in it. With Vibriosis, changing the water and cleaning the substrate are the two most important tasks.

Using an effect detritus pack is also essential, as these nasty bacteria eat uneaten food and waste material. They then thrive and are in turn eaten by the fish. For this reason, it is also very important not to overfeed your fish so there is no uneaten food floating around.

Finally, keeping fish stress-free and using good quality food will keep your Clownfish's immune systems strong, which will make it easier for them to resist infection.

L) Ammonia Poisoning and Ammonia Burn

As the name implies, these are not illnesses or diseases but medical conditions caused by levels of ammonia in tank water that are far too high.

These elevated levels are usually due to equipment malfunction or failure, loss of power, when too many new marine creatures are introduced at one time and filters can't cope or when healthy bacteria in the tank have been lost as a result of medications in the water or sudden changes to water parameters.

Symptoms

With ammonia poisoning, the fish's gills become red and inflamed. Breathing is difficult and the fish gasps for air, often remaining at the surface of the water in an effort to ease the situation. Badly poisoned fish loose their appetites, become lethargic and may just lie on the bottom of the tank. Clamped fins may also be a symptom.

In the advanced stages of poisoning, red streaks and patches appear on the skin and fins. These begin to bleed, as do the gills. As tissues are further broken down the fish begins to haemorrhage internally too and also suffers damage to the central nervous system. Fish suffering ammonia poisoning will die if it is not treated very early.

With ammonia burn, there is redness and inflammation on the fins and tail.

Treatment

Treatment involves replacing 25 to 50 % of the water in the aquarium. In addition, the pH must be lowered so that the level is below 7.0.

Fish that have been very badly poisoned can't be treated and will die. Euthanasia is a kinder option.

Prevention

The best methods to prevent ammonia poisoning and burn are to test the water regularly, avoid overcrowding in the tank, do regular water changes and make sure that all the essential equipment is working at all times. By doing these things, your fish won't become victims of this destructive chemical compound.

M) Dropsy

Dropsy is a symptom of a gram-negative bacterial infection of some kind and it is not a disease or illness in and of itself. Bacterial infections are more common in fish with weak immune systems caused by stress from transportation, poor water quality including high ammonia or nitrate levels, inadequate nutrition or a marked drop in the temperature of the water.

Symptoms

The typical symptoms of dropsy are a very swollen or distended belly or abdomen and scales that stand out from the body. The scales can stick out almost at right angles to the body and can make the fish look a little like a pinecone.

There are numerous symptoms caused by the underlying infections but these two are due to Dropsy itself.

Treatment

It is not easy to treat Dropsy usually because the underlying infection causing it is so far advanced by this stage. As a result, some aquarists believe that the kindest thing to do is to euthanize affected fish.

Treatment of Dropsy must, in effect, be one for the underlying bacterial condition. Affected fish must be placed in a quarantine tank and, once the bacteria concerned has been identified, dosed with a suitable antibiotic. The water's salinity levels are raised too (1 teaspoon per gallon is recommended).

A water change must be performed on the main tank to reduce the number of bacteria that may be present.

Prevention

In order to prevent Dropsy, one must prevent bacterial infections. The golden rule with that is to maintain a high level of water quality by performing all the necessary maintenance tasks. Avoiding overfeeding and overcrowding is also important, as is a healthy and varied diet for all fish.

N) Hole in the Head (HITH) / Head and Lateral Line Erosion (HLLE)

The cause for this illness is not yet known or understood. The three most popular theories are that HITH or HLLE are caused by poor nutrition, long-term use of filters that use activated carbon and, finally, poor water quality. Other aquarists think that a lack of vitamins is a further contributing factor.

Symptoms

Fish suffering from HLLE develop indentations along the lateral line and on the head. It looks as though the tissue is breaking down. These indentations or pits worsen into holes or even open wounds, which can then become infected by bacteria. These fish loose their appetites and become very lethargic.

This condition progresses slowly and is not fatal. However, the effects on the fish's appetite and the secondary infections as a result of the HLLE are the killers.

Treatment

HLLE requires a broad treatment approach because the causes are unknown. One therefore needs to cover all the possibilities:

- Do a water change and perform them regularly

- Ensure that their diet is optimal

- Add vitamins (Vitamins A, D, and E or the B range) or vitamin enriched foods to their diet

- Iodine can also be a helpful supplement

- Use antibiotics *if* the fish is suffering from a secondary infection

- If you use carbon-based filtration either rinse it out very well or stop using it.

O) Nitrite / Nitrate Poisoning

Nitrate or Nitrite poisoning is also called Brown Blood Disease. As the name indicates, this is not a disease but a serious and potentially fatal medical condition brought about by fish being affected/poisoned by elevated levels of nitrates in the water.

One of the lead causes of Nitrate/Nitrite poisoning is a bio-load that is far heavier than the filtration and other tank systems can cope with or following a failure of the filtration system or a prolonged power loss.

Symptoms

There is a range of symptoms that will assist a tank owner to diagnose this form of poisoning in fish even if testing the nitrate levels in the tank is not enough to indicate this.

The milder symptoms include lethargy and very limited movement with affected fish tending to stay just below the water surface. Poisoned fish gasp for air and may remain near the surface or water outlets. The gills move very rapidly and loose their normal pink or red colour and turn brown.

The name Brown Blood Disease stems from the increase in levels of methemoglobin in the blood, which literally turns it brown. The even more serious aspect of this rise in methemoglobin is that blood becomes unable to transport oxygen. Fish, in effect, suffocate to death. It also results in damage to, and loss of, blood cells and organ damage too.

Treatment

The single most important intervention is an immediate water change. Nitrate levels must be tested and watched very closely. Further partial water changes must be done as necessary. In fact, more water changes are necessary the larger the population of the tank.

One also needs to increase the rate of aeration and add chlorine salt (ideally) or aquarium salt to the water. If the affected fish are not eating well, or at all, you must reduce the amount of food you put in the tank. Uneaten food will add to the problems. This regimen must be continued until you get nitrate readings of zero.

Prevention

Performing the necessary routine maintenance, not over feeding or overstocking and testing nitrate levels regularly are the very best ways to prevent a lethal build-up of this toxic compound in the tank water.

In the case of a new tank, the stock should be introduced slowly so that the systems can adjust and accommodate them and toxic compounds such as nitrates don't begin to build up. Levels should be tested regularly.

A red flag for nitrate level problems is an increase in ammonia levels. If your tests pick up raised ammonia there is every chance that, unless you take immediate corrective steps, a nitrate increase will follow very soon.

P) Oxygen Starvation

While poisoning results from an intake of a harmful substance, this condition is the result of fish not getting enough oxygen due to inadequate water aeration or gas exchange at the surface of the water.

Symptoms

As would be expected with a lack of oxygen, the main symptom is that affected fish will gasp for air, sometimes with their mouths above the surface of the water. Fish often appear to be gulping and the gills move very quickly.

Treatment

The most obvious 'fix' is to increase the levels of aeration, and therefore oxygen, in the tank by increasing airflow and the speed of water circulation through the filters.

Aquarists also suggest that one check the water temperature. If the temperature goes up, the oxygen requirements go up too. If you find that the water is too warm it's vital to bring it down to normal levels as quickly as possible. Using the cooling or chilling methods described in an earlier chapter will prove useful and will bring relief to the fish as oxygen becomes available in the water once more.

Q) External Bubble Disease

This condition is not infectious and is due entirely to one of two environmental factors: too much oxygen or too much water pressure.

The symptoms are dramatic and alarming but often the condition resolves itself. If it doesn't it can be treated and managed fairly easily.

Symptoms

As the name suggests, the main symptom are gas-filled bubbles that are clearly visible and form on the outside of the fish's body or on the eyes or fins. In extreme cases the bubbles are so large that the fish floats, unable to swim.

Although fish that are affected by Bubble Disease can suffer permanent damage to the skin, eyes (even loss of an eye or blindness) or fins, it is not often a fatal condition. The exception is when bubbles also form internally, as they can cause organs to rupture or fail. This is rare, fortunately. The other complicating factor is bacterial infections in tissue after the bubbles have popped.

Treatment

The treatment that is administered is dependent on which of the two causes are responsible for the formation of these bubbles. In either case, however, the bubbles must *not* be popped as this leaves the fish vulnerable to infection as it causes an opening into the skin, fin or eye, and it causes pain!

If the cause is oxygen super-saturation, the water temperature in the tank probably needs to be raised. Although it won't happen immediately, the warming water will release the extra oxygen into the air above the water surface. One needs to monitor the temperature very carefully so that the water does not become too warm as this will stress the fish and also drop oxygen levels too low which will then lead to oxygen starvation and suffocation.

If, on the other hand, the condition is due to pressure, one needs to depressurise the fish. This is usually only found in wild-caught fish that were living at depth and were brought to the surface too fast. The bubbles of oxygen in their bodies are forced to the surface where they form bubbles.

In the unlikely event of a Clownfish with pressure induced Bubble Disease, you need to place it as deep in the aquarium as you can and keep in at that depth until the symptoms begin to ease.

Prevention

The best way to guard against Bubble Disease in Clownfish is to buy captive-bred specimens and to ensure that water temperatures and oxygen/aeration levels are as they should be at all times.

3) A fish First Aid Kit

While one can't prepare for every eventuality, it is a good idea to keep a first aid kit on hand so you can treat your Clownfish and other marine creatures immediately if the need arises. Some illnesses are so aggressive that waiting for your vet or a shop to open the next day or Monday morning is simply not an option!

A marine tank First Aid Kit should include the following items:

- A refractometer
- Measuring equipment such as syringes and / or pipettes
- A copper test kit
- A suitably sized, soft gauze aquarium net
- Medications:
    o Formalin solution
    o Methylene Blue
    o A copper-based product
    o Malachite Green
    o An antibacterial agent
    o A deworming agent.

There is a range of these products available. Your vet or a specialist retailer will be able to advise you as to which would be best for your tank and requirements.

It's important to check the contents of the kit regularly to make sure that none of the medications or solutions are past their expiry dates. If they are they must be replaced immediately. In addition, as you finish something you need to purchase more. You don't want to discover you have run out of a life-saving item at the time you really need it!

A quarantine tank is of course a very big part of a tank owner's ability to prevent health problems and deal effectively with them when, not if, they do occur.

4) Pet insurance

If you use a quarantine tank, follow good maintenance routines and schedules to ensure high quality water, and use high quality foods to strengthen immunity your Clownfish and other tank inhabitants should stay pretty healthy. However, marine fish are prone to illness and even the healthiest marine creature can be injured.

Enter pet insurance. It used to be that pet insurance only catered for dogs and cats. In a very recent development, there are now some insurers that will cover fish. One would have to establish which companies offer this option and whether it covers marine fish and not just goldfish in bowels.

With standard insurance, there is a choice of a plan that covers expenses in the event of an accident only. Others will pay costs for both accident and illness. Your vet should be able to supply you with a brochure, pamphlet or information. You will have to weigh the cost of insurance against the possibility of being out of pocket at a later date.

Like most insurance, these policies will have a deductible or excess that you will have to pay, but they can help greatly if your marine creatures ever require vet care in the form of tests and/or medications. The premium and affordability will also vary depending on the type of cover chosen.

Chapter 12: Breeding Clownfish

Clownfish were one of the very first marine fish species to be bred commercially, and captive breeding of these popular fish has been very successful.

Some breeders say that if you want to breed your Clownfish, you need a pair or a mated pair. That is not always possible, though. As previously discussed, the gender and gender changes – or lack of them – in Clownfish is complex. To accommodate this, other breeders advise those who want to start breeding this species to purchase 6 or more fish as this almost certainly guarantees that one will end up with a breeding pair.

Once you have your breeding pair, there are things you can do to encourage them to spawn – such as keeping the quality of the water high – and, later, ways to help as many of the hatchlings to survive as possible. Once the mating pair starts the cycle, the female will lay eggs every 12 to 18 days.

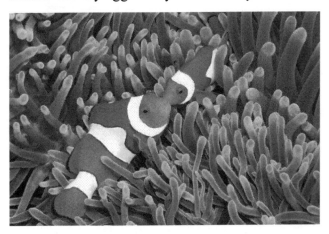

1) Sexual maturity

Once you have a mating pair of Clownfish, they will need to be in a stable tank environment that offers them good quality water for anything from a few months to a year before they spawn for the first time.

Once they begin, however, spawning will occur frequently and at regular and therefore predictable intervals. In the wild, the Clownfish's reproductive cycle often correlates with the lunar cycle. The spawning rates peak around the first and third quarters of the moon. This means that the eggs will hatch around the full moon or new moon periods when the tides are at their highest and predation may be at its lowest. Clownfish in captivity may also be affected by the moon but this is not a common phenomenon.

2) Spawning

Clownfish start to act differently around spawning time. The female suddenly gets fatter or thicker in the middle of her body and this may well be an indication that she is 'pregnant' or carrying eggs. Spawning nearly always takes place in the late afternoon.

When it is time to spawn, the male and female begin to build a nest by using their fins and mouths to clear a section of rock near their host anemone (if there is one). The male will then court the female. During courtship, he 'dances' up and down, waggles his body and extends and displays his fins. He also chases the female and nips at her, as if herding or guiding her, until she enters the nest area.

A small tube can be seen protruding from the body of both the male and the female. The eggs and sperm respectively will emerge from these tubes. A spawning female swims back and forth on the cleaned or nest section of the rock. With each pass, she lays and deposits eggs. When the male gets his turn, he too swims back and forth over the eggs and deposits sperm, which then fertilizes the eggs.

Both the male and the female Clownfish stop frequently in order to aerate the eggs by blowing on them with their mouths. Each spawning session usually lasts for approximately an hour. At the end of it, the eggs remain stuck to the rock of the nest. These newly laid eggs look orange or yellow.

The female lays anything between 600 and 1500 eggs at one time. The eggs in the nest are fertilised externally by the male. The male then guards and cares for the eggs for several days (usually 6 to 10 days) until they hatch.

3) Caring for the eggs

The male is fiercely protective of the clutch. He will remain with the eggs, aggressively and fearlessly chasing off any potential predators regardless of their size and nipping at them. This behaviour will be extended to the tank owner if fingers get too close!

Dead or infertile eggs are carefully removed from the clutch by the male using his mouth. In addition, he mouths the viable or healthy eggs. He also keeps the nest site clear of debris and fans the eggs often to achieve this and to keep them oxygenated.

This fanning of the eggs is a very important and interesting factor. According to several studies, eggs develop and hatch faster in clutches that have been fanned regularly. This would seem to indicate that the male can control the speed and overall success of hatching.

Male Clownfish and fanning behaviour may also be affected by environmental factors in the wild. For example, if conditions are not optimal, he may not fan the eggs much at all in order to decrease the number of hatchlings or slow hatching down until conditions are better.

The female Clownfish does not care for the eggs the way the male does. However, she patrols nearby and will aggressively defend the clutch. She is even more territorial and aggressive than the male at this time.

Clownfish eggs change colour and look almost silvery as they develop. The eyes of the embryos in the eggs become visible after about 5 days. These changes and evidence of growth trigger even more active and vigilant care from the male who moves over them and fans are cleans them almost 24 hours a day at this stage.

4) *The hatching tank*

Some aquarists believe that when Clownfish eggs turn silver in colour, they will hatch that night. However, given it is best not to allow the eggs to hatch in the main tank, where they will most likely be eaten by corals or other fish, you need to ideally remove the eggs about two days before they hatch and place them in a dedicated tank.

A hatching or rearing tank only needs to be a small (10 gallons or 45.5 UK litres or 37 US litres), although you can use a larger one if you choose to do so. These tanks, like quarantine tanks, can be sparse in terms of equipment. All that is necessary is a heater or heating mat, a small air-stone and a pump. There is no need for substrate or any tank décor.

A light is also important because the eyesight of Clownfish fry is poor and they need to eat a lot and must be able to find the food. The light, however, should not be too bright. It is essential that you don't install a filter or filtration system of any kind in a hatching tank. The babies are very small and delicate and filters will injure or even kill them.

What is essential is that the pH level and temperature of the water are as close to those in the main tank as possible. Some aquarists recommend that one exchange half of the fresh water from the hatching tank with that of the main aquarium so that the water conditions are as close as possible.

You also need to be able to black out the tank to allow hatching, as the eggs will only hatch in the dark. Nothing sophisticated is needed for this, as one can achieve a black-out by draping the tank with blankets or some other fabric that is thick enough to exclude light.

Once the hatching tank is ready, it is time to transfer the eggs into it from the main tank. The ideal scenario is removing the eggs along with the rock they are on. Because the eggs must not come into contact with air, you need to place the rock into a suitable transfer container under the water.

Ideally, the rock on which the eggs are should be positioned at an angle – the steeper the better – against the side of the tank. Good water circulation is necessary for the eggs but the air-stone shouldn't be so close that the eggs and the bubbles make contact. Once the stone and eggs are in position, the blanket or fabric should be placed over the tank so no light penetrates it.

The tank must be left covered and undisturbed for a minimum of two hours, during which time the eggs should hatch. It's essential to resist the urge to sneak a peak because the eggs won't hatch if there is light, even if only for a brief period. Any light causes the eggs to become inactive and they may only hatch the following night.

Of course, removing the rock complete with its eggs from the main aquarium won't be possible or practical if the breeding pair laid their eggs on a large live rock in your aquarium! In order to avoid a problem of this sort in the future, you could consider placing a tile or a flat or near-flat piece of pottery where your Clownfish usually spawn. The Clownfish will lay their eggs on the surface you provide. A tile or piece of pottery can be removed very easily from the tank when hatching is imminent without disrupting the tank at all.

In the event that the eggs hatch in the main tank, you will have to remove the Clownfish larvae or fry. The first important step is to turn off all the pumps and filters in the main tank. It's important that there is no current or flow and no risk that these tiny little babies could be sucked into filter or skimmer pipes etc. Next, switch the tank lights off and, after approximately 30 minutes, shine a bright light into the water. Don't shine the torch onto the eggs in case there are still some that are yet to hatch.

The hatchlings will find the light irresistible and will swim towards it. The next stage of the process is easier if you have someone who can help you by holding the light for you. You need to start a siphon and begin siphoning the Clownfish fry. It's often easier to place them into a temporary container and then pour them into the hatching tank.

5) Hatching

In the wild, things are naturally very different! When a Clownfish hatches, it rises up through the water towards the surface of the sea where it drifts for a week or two. At this stage the baby fish is a tiny and transparent larva and does not remotely resemble a fish.

The next stage is when it grows and develops and, during those first couple of weeks, it changes into a Clownfish that is less than half an inch (1.25 centimetres) long. This little fish then swims or drifts down to a reef where it will seek out a host anemone. If it is unable to find one within a day or two, it will die.

Even in captivity, it is the fragile larval stage that is critical. This phase lasts on average 10 days but may be a little more or less. If the hobbyist can nurse the hatchlings through this stage, the hardest part is done and the chances of the young Clownfish surviving is good.

However, even experienced aquarists are not able to successfully raise all the fry. It's a difficult thing to do but breeders suggest that one select 10 to 20 strong-looking hatchlings to concentrate on. Many fry won't live longer than 24 hours in any event. One needs to siphon out all the dead, deformed and weak fry.

The behaviour of dying fry or baby Clownfish is hard to miss. They struggle to swim and may just spin in currents in the tank. Others will simply sink to the bottom of the tank, try to swim and then sink again.

Fry or hatchlings behaving in this manner are unlikely to survive for more than a day. Either a siphon pipe or a pipette can be used to remove the dead or dying young.

Healthy, just hatched Clownfish will be very hungry. One way to boost the survival rate is to place food such as Rotifers in the hatching tank so the babies can begin to feed immediately. This food must be live food and of a size that the fry can manage.

6) Feeding Clownfish larvae and fry

Newly hatched Clownfish must have live food. If one uses flake foods, the babies will starve to death and the water will fill with uneaten food. The ideal food for Clownfish that are at the larvae stage is Rotifers, which are minute aquatic animals or zooplankton that contain vitamins that are essential for survival and healthy growth. As the fish get bigger, Brine Shrimp are added to the diet.

Rotifers must be added to the hatching tank water as quickly as possible because the larvae will begin to eat 12 to 24 hours after hatching when they have used all the nutrients from the yolk sac. The larvae won't swim far to get food, which means that it's very important that there are Rotifers throughout the tank. This can be a fine balance, though, because one doesn't want to overstock with these zooplankton and compromise water quality.

For the first 4 or 5 days of their lives, the babies will need to be fed every 2 to 3 hours, day and night. This feeding schedule is a little demanding for the tank owner but the rewards are great: strong, healthy and brightly coloured Clownfish! Paler coloured fish are very often the result of inadequate feeding at the very early stages of life.

Given the fry are small and the Rotifers are microscopic, you will only know your babies are eating by observing their behaviour. If you observe a baby fish swim, stop, curve its tail and then dart forward at high speed you know it is eating, as that is the feeding technique of Clownfish fry.

Following the 4 or 5 days of regular feedings of Rotifers, the fry will be large enough to eat live Brine Shrimp as well. These shrimp are a highly nutritious when they have recently hatched because they have a yolk sac attached to them. It is therefore both the shrimp and the egg sac that are so beneficial for the rapidly growing Clownfish fry. Brine Shrimp that are older than a few days are far less nutritious because the yolk sac has been absorbed by the growing shrimp.

After 5 or 6 days, feeding frequency can be reduced to every 4 to 6 hours. What you need to check for is that the fry have distended, orange-looking, and full stomachs at all times. It is thought that if they have empty stomachs at this early and important stage of their growth and development, the stomach lining can fuse to itself, making feeding difficult or even impossible.

From day 9 onwards the fry can move to a diet of Brine Shrimp and crushed flake food. Keep in mind that you only want to feed the live shrimp and not the egg shells or casings.

In summary:

- *Days 1 to 5*: feed the larval Clownfish Rotifers only, every 2 to 3 hours

- *Days 5 to 8*: feed the fish Rotifers and Brine Shrimp every 4 to 6 hours

- *Day 9 onwards*: feed the fry Brine Shrimp and crushed marine fish flakes every 4 to 6 hours.

7) Breeding food for fry

Ideally, an aquarist should breed the food that Clownfish at the larval and fry stages need. Doing so can sometimes be trickier than raising the fish! Rotifers can be a little tricky to breed or culture, but they do reproduce very quickly (they double in numbers about every 24 hours) and are essential for raising your baby fish. A Rotifer culture should be started a week before the eggs are due to hatch.

Rotifers

The two most frequently used Rotifer species are *Brachionus plicatilis* and *Brachionus rotundiformis*. They feed on a few species of microalgae/single-celled marine algae, which can be purchased from specialist marine aquarium suppliers and retailers. The species of microalgae that are most often recommended to feed Rotifers are *Nannochlopsis*, *Isochrysis galbana* or *Pavlova lutheri*.

In order to successfully culture Rotifers to feed to your Clownfish larvae, you will need certain equipment:

- Rotifer culture
- Rotifer food
- 5 gallon (22.75 UK litres or 18.5 US litres) bucket
- Air-stone
- Air pump
- Plastic airline Tubing
- Rotifer sieve or coffee filter papers.

While it is very important that there is water circulation in the bucket, the airflow from the air-stone should be set low so that there are only a few bubbles.

Mix salt water in the bucket, taking care to match the specific gravity of the water in the bag the Rotifers are in. The salinity level is usually approximately 1.017. Don't add the Rotifers until the water is well mixed and you have checked the specific gravity.

The next item to be added to the bucket is the Rotifer food. This should not simply be dumped into the bucket but added to the water a drop at a time. Stop adding the food when the water turns a light green colour.

This colour should be preserved at all times. If the water is not light green it means there is not enough food in the bucket for the Rotifers. The colour and by extension the food levels must be checked every day.

One should not harvest any Rotifers for the first 3 or 4 days so that they have a chance to reproduce or multiply and reach large numbers in the water. When it is time to harvest them, you should remove about a third of the Rotifers each day so they continue to multiply. Harvesting Rotifers is not complex.

- Slowly and carefully pour about one third of the total volume of water from the bucket through a coffee filter or a Rotifer sieve.

- Dip the coffee filter or sieve into the water of the hatching tank and very gently soak or rinse the Rotifers into the water.

Even after you no longer need Rotifers for Clownfish food, you should go on harvesting them in order to keep the culture healthy and ready for when you need them again.

The water in the Rotifers' tank or container must be changed weekly after they have been harvested. The water must always contain enough food to sustain both the Rotifers and the light green colour. If the colour fades, it indicates there is insufficient food for the Rotifers in the water.

Brine Shrimp

One can buy Brine Shrimp hatcheries, most of which consist of a stand and a pipe, so that a small aerator can be attached. The final item one needs to use is a two litre (½ gallon) plastic bottle or other suitable container. Marine retailers supply packets of Brine Shrimp eggs and salt for inclusion in the water.

The container should be filled to a few inches below the rim. The supplied salt should be mixed into prepared water. Once the aerator hose has been placed into the container, one can simply pour the Brine Shrimp eggs into the water. The eggs will hatch in 24 to 48 hours.

The shells left behind after Brine Shrimp have hatched are brown and they float, often to the surface of the water in the hatchery. The hatched shrimps, on the other hand, stay at the bottom. This makes it much easier to remove the shells, which can't and shouldn't be used as food. The eggs can be skimmed off using a suitable net or a pipette.

The Brine Shrimp that you have grown should only be kept for 3 or 4 few days after they have hatched. This means that you need to place eggs in the hatchery on a staggered basis so that there are always newly hatched shrimp for your Clownfish fry to eat.

8) Growing hatchlings

You now have a hatching tank containing young Clownfish and you are culturing Rotifers and Brine Shrimp and keeping the young fish well fed. What else do you need to do to keep the growing fry healthy and strong?

As with the main tank or aquarium, regular water changes are essential. Aquarists recommend that 25% of the water in the hatching tank be replaced every day or second day. Water salinity levels and temperature must be monitored and controlled and top-off and new water must be correctly prepared or the young will die of shock.

When the fry are about 10 days old and showing adult colours they need to be moved to a "growing-on" tank that is larger than the hatching tank. A tank of 20 gallons (91 litres UK or 76 litres US) is suggested for this purpose. This tank should preferably have a filter that is fitted under a gravel substrate.

The growing-on tank must be prepared and it should be allowed to settle for several days before the fry are transferred to it. 25% of the water in the growing-on tank should be replaced every 2 to 4 days in order to maintain high water quality and guard against infections etc. This tank should be home to strongest and biggest fry.

Even these stronger babies must be handled with extreme care to avoid injuries. Nets are not advised; rather use a cup or another suitably-sized container or a plastic bag. The less developed and weaker fry can then remain in the hatching tank a little longer and until they are more robust.

The fry in the growing-on tank should be fed a more varied and adult diet.

9) Re-homing baby Clownfish

Raising Clownfish fry is a lot of work but managing to do so successfully is really exciting and very rewarding. However, what if you can't or don't want to keep them all?

You really only have two options. You can sell them privately but this presents real problems unless you know how to safely ship fish. The second option is to approach a dealer. Marine retailers are often interested in acquiring healthy Clownfish when they are about 0.5 inches or 1.25 centimetres.

On the down side, you are unlikely to be paid much for them. An alternative that some breeders opt for is to be given credit or goods by the supplier in exchange for fry.

Chapter 13: Prices, costs & where to buy Clownfish

1) Costs

The cost to purchase a Clownfish:

These amazing fish do not come cheap! A Clownfish will set you back between £20 / $30 and £80 / $118 and the rarer, more exotic species can cost £150 / $222. On top of that, you will need to pay for all the equipment you will need before you can even take your new pet home.

Set-up costs:

You need certain basic equipment for your Clownfish. These once-off costs include:

- Tank or aquarium: depending on size and design the prices range from $55 / £37 to $2000 / £1349. Some of these prices include a hood or cover and an under-substrate filter. The very expensive tanks may include housing such as a cabinet and a number of pieces of equipment.
- Substrate: $9 – 39 / £6 – 26
- Live rocks: $22 – 30 / £15 – 20
- Live sand: $34 / £23
- Coral: $4.50 – 33 / £3 – 22
- Algae sheets or attack pack: $3 – 16 / £2 – 11
- Filter: $ 5.50 – 25 / £4 – 17
- Calcium reactor: $190 – 312 / £128 – 211
- Thermometer: $2.75 – 18 / £1.85 – 12
- Air-stone: $2.50 – 18 / £1.60 – 12
- Powerhead: $22 – 70 / £15 – 47
- Wave makers and oscillators: $176 – 296 / £119 – 200
- Air pump: $12 – 85 / £8 – 57
- Heater: $29 – 38.50 / £ 19 – 26
- Protein skimmer: $89 – 281 / £60 – 190

- Full spectrum light: $6 – 296 / £4 – 200
- Water conditioner: $2 – 13 / £1.35 – 9
- Hydrometer: $9 – 17 / £6 – 11.25
- Refractometer: $12 / £8
- Detritus attack pack: $39 – 160 / £26.30 – 108
- Water test kit: $14.50 – 40 / £10 – 27
- Water filter: $13 – 150 / £8.50 – 101
- Carbon filtration system: $89 – 218 / £60 – 147.50
- Reverse Osmosis (RO) or Deionization (DI) filtration unit: $123 – 388 / £83 – 262
- UV Steriliser: $16 – 297 / £11 – 200

These are just for a single tank or aquarium. Additional tanks and a few of the most basic items will be necessary for a hatching, growing-on and quarantine tank.

You may be able to buy items, including second-hand or pre-owned ones, more cheaply online but then you need to think about how clean these items might be. The last thing you want is to acquire a tank that is infected with bacteria, a virus or a parasite that will infect all your stock.

Ongoing, regular costs:

These expenses include all the items you need for regular, routine maintenance and hygiene and for the overall health and well being of your Clownfish and other marine tank inhabitants.

- Aquarium salt mix: $22 – 74 / £15 – 50
- Limewater: $18 – 21 / £12 – 14
- Aquarium nets: $4 – 6 / £3 – 4
- Aquarium brushes: $11 / £7.50
- Marine flake food: $5 – 11 / £3.30 – 7.25
- Krill: $3 / £1.80
- Shrimp or Mysis: $5 – 10 / £3.15 – 7
- Spirulina flakes: $6 / £4.25
- Rotifers: $13 / £8.75
- Rotifer feed: $8 – 16 / £5.40 – 10.80
- Brine Shrimp eggs: $12 – 16 / £8 – 10.80

These regular costs obviously don't include any emergencies or unforeseen 'extras' that you may encounter such as vet bills for tests, for example.

2) *Where you can buy a Clownfish*

Buying equipment from more general or non-specialist retailers is usually fine. However, one needs to be careful about where one buys the fish themselves.

One doesn't want to obtain specimens that are sold as captive-bred but are in actual fact wild caught. In addition, less specialised retailers may, deliberately or inadvertently, sell fish that are close to the end of their life span or sick.

You could ask a vet who includes fish in his or her practise for recommendations about local breeders. In addition, do research on the Internet. Joining Clownfish groups, clubs and forums online is a wonderful way to find information.

There are shops that one can visit and a large number of reputable online marine specialist shops where one can buy fish that will be shipped safely.

Chapter 14: Conclusion

1) Do's… in no particular order

- ✓ Learn about Clownfish and marine aquarium care

- ✓ Find out what fish and other species are compatible and can share a tank

- ✓ Make sure you get a tank that is large enough

- ✓ Buy captive-bred fish rather than wild-caught fish

- ✓ Observe fish carefully to look for signs of ill health before buying a fish

- ✓ Cure live rocks before placing them in the aquarium

- ✓ Take the time to set up the aquarium or tank properly

- ✓ Include an algae attack pack

- ✓ Make use of a detritus attack pack

- ✓ Invest in good quality tank equipment

- ✓ Buy and equip a smaller tank that will be used as a quarantine or hospital tank

- ✓ Ensure that the water quality of always good

- ✓ Draw up a maintenance schedule

- ✓ Perform regular maintenance

- ✓ Check and meet all the necessary water and tank parameters (salinity, pH, temperature, calcium, phosphates, etc.)

- ✓ Take the time to acclimate all marine creatures using either the float or the drip method before placing them in a tank

- ✓ Deal with salt creep

- ✓ Be prepared for a loss of power

- ✓ Feed Clownfish a diet that includes vegetable matter

- ✓ Keep a First Aid Kit

- ✓ Quarantine corals

- ✓ Only feed larvae and fry live food in the form of Rotifers and Brine Shrimp.

2) Don'ts… in no particular order

- Use tap water

- Use common table salt

- Fail to test water parameters regularly

- Neglect routine maintenance tasks including performing water replacements

- Introduce uncured live rocks in the aquarium

- Rush the vital acclimation process

- Feed Clownfish frozen food

- Overfeed fish

- Place too many fish in a tank so you have over crowding which causes stress

- Ignore signs of ill health

- Neglect to make contingency plans for in the event of a power failure

- Leave fish unattended in the treatment bath or the dip

- Feed fry Brine Shrimp eggs.

3) A reminder of the Big Mistakes that cost!

One needs to take being a Clownfish owner seriously. This commitment must begin before you even bring your new pet home. These creatures are entirely dependent on the tank owner and he or she can't decide to take a few days off or go away without making provision for the care of the aquarium.

An aquarium is a "closed system" and without due care, the marine creatures in it will not survive. An aquarist or hobbyist must take the time and trouble to become informed by learning about the species and about caring for marine or saltwater tanks.

The main reason that fish die in tanks – as a rule – is because owners are either ignorant or don't care for the inhabitants properly. The primary causes of aquarium fish death are:

Improper or no acclimation

It's not enough to acclimate new fish to water temperature alone because this is just one of the important environmental factors. Fish also need to be acclimated to the pH. The shock of a sudden change in pH can kill fish that are particularly sensitive to this particular parameter.

Incorrect diet or insufficient food

If fish, like any other living creature, don't receive enough food, they will become malnourished and weak. Their immune systems are then affected and fish are far less likely to be able to fend off or fight an infection or infestation. If there is no food provided, fish will starve to death rapidly, especially very young fish.

In addition to not being given enough food, being fed the wrong diet is also a big problem. Either the fish simply won't eat a food item that they are unfamiliar with or can't cope with or they will eat it and be adversely affected by it.

Contamination of the aquarium and stock

Not using a quarantine tank can be disastrous. Fish may appear healthy and a retailer may supply specimens in good faith but they may be carrying parasites including ones that cause very serious illness such as Cryptocaryon and Oodinium. Not only will the infected fish require treatment, which may or may not be successful, but all the fish in the tank might become infected.

Using a quarantine tank will usually save your fish from illness and suffering and you from a great deal of work, expense and distress.

Poor water quality

Fish must have a stable environment that stays within certain set parameters. These are non-negotiable and include the correct levels or total absence of certain compounds, pH and salinity levels, oxygenation levels and temperature. Not testing these parameters regularly will prove very costly to you and your fish and other marine creatures.

If water is not of high quality, the fish become stressed and this weakens their immune systems and their systems generally. This leaves them vulnerable to attack by bacteria, viruses and parasites.

Good water quality is not difficult to maintain if one prepares water properly and carries out all of the necessary maintenance tasks including the very important partial water changes correctly and regularly. This would also include ensuring that vital equipment such as filters and skimmers are working, as they should.

Species incompatibility

Not all Clownfish species get on well together because they are fairly territorial, even aggressive, fish. In addition, some Clownfish only get on well with a limited number of other kinds of fish.

Part of the all-important homework that must be done before setting up an aquarium is to examine compatibility so that the residents of your aquarium get on and don't attack each other or become stressed.

4) And in closing...

This guide's primary purpose is to make sure that you have the information that you need to decide, first and foremost, if this is really the right pet for you, for your spouse, or for your child.

If the answer is a confident and honest "Yes", this pet owner's guide will also give you the details that will help you to keep your Clownfish healthy and happy.

All animals in captivity should at least live to their usual or expected life span. In fact, given they are safe from their natural predators and receive a good diet and vet care, they should exceed the average life span for their species.

If you are one of those individuals who commits to owning and caring for one of these amazing fish, you will be rewarded by having a pet that is fascinating, beautiful, and rewarding! Enjoy your Clownfish and teach others about them.

Published by AAX Publishing 2015

Made in the USA
Columbia, SC
08 December 2022

73021725R00074